THE Boyhood
Ranald Bannerman

D0547084

GEORGE MACDONALD (1824-1905) was a Scottish preacher, novelist, and poet. He wrote more than fifty books, including the classic fantasies *At the Back of the North Wind, The Princess and the Goblin,* and *The Princess and Curdie. The Boyhood of Ranald Bannerman* has been "lost" for 75 years, and is here made available for a new generation of readers.

DAN HAMILTON, a freelance writer, enjoys the writings of George MacDonald, C.S. Lewis, J.R.R. Tolkien, Charles Williams, and G.K. Chesterton. Dan, his wife Elizabeth, and their daughter Jennifer live in Indianapolis.

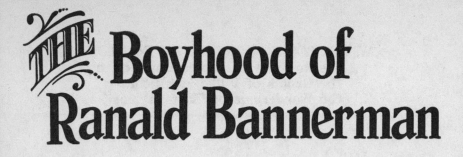

The Boyhood of Ranald Bannerman

GEORGE MACDONALD

Edited for today's young reader by
DAN HAMILTON

A WINNER BOOK

VICTOR BOOKS™
A DIVISION OF SCRIPTURE PRESS PUBLICATIONS INC.
USA CANADA ENGLAND

WINNER BOOKS BY GEORGE MACDONALD:
The Boyhood of Ranald Bannerman
The Genius of Willie MacMichael
The Wanderings of Clare Skymer

Library of Congress Catalog Card Number: 86-63104
ISBN: 0-89693-748-8

VICTOR BOOKS
A division of SP Publications, Inc.
Wheaton, Illinois 60187

CONTENTS

EDITOR'S FOREWORD

George MacDonald wrote his many books for the childlike of all ages—for any man, woman, boy, or girl who would receive God, the things of God, and the things of God's world with open hands, warm hearts, and simple faith.

The Boyhood of Ranald Bannerman is one such book, originally published in 1869 as *Ranald Bannerman's Boyhood.* In telling this tale, MacDonald drew many of the people, places, events, thoughts, and lessons from his own boyhood and adventures. In particular, his portrait of Mr. Bannerman reflects the love of his own father as his key to understanding the love of God.

Like many other writers of his time, MacDonald did have his technical faults. He often composed awkward and intricate sentences, repeated himself, sermonized, lost track of minor details, and sometimes wandered away from his subject. Yet he was a true *storyteller,* and always left his readers turning pages to see what would happen next. His narrative skill was matched by the wise quality of his spiritual insights, for MacDonald spun his tales in order to tell us all about our Heavenly Father, His Son Jesus Christ, and the unbounded love with which They seek to persuade us to turn from our sins.

This special edition has been trimmed from the original and edited for the enjoyment of today's younger reader. It retains the rich essence and wonder of MacDonald's story and his penetrating, godly insights, but corrects some of his writing flaws and is easier to read.

May this edition bring all its readers delight in a "new"

author, and spur a growing interest in MacDonald at his fullest and best. And may such interest warrant the eventual reprinting of his complete, original works.

DAN HAMILTON

CHAPTER ONE

The Glimmer of Twilight

I, Ranald Bannerman, am a Scotchman. My father was the clergyman of a country parish in northern Scotland—a humble position, involving plain living and plain ways. We lived on a glebe or church-farm attached to the manse, or clergyman's house. My father rented a small farm besides, for he needed all he could make by farming to supplement his small salary.

My mother was an invalid, hence she was unable to spend much time with us four boys. She is very beautiful in my memory, but during the last months of her life we seldom saw her. The desire to keep the house quiet for her sake must have been the beginning of that outdoor freedom which we enjoyed the whole of our boyhood.

My oldest memories are of dreams. One in particular I dreamed often. It was of the room I slept in, only it was narrower and loftier. The window was gone, and the sun, moon, and stars lived in the ceiling.

The sun was not a scientific sun at all, but had a round, jolly man's face. And the moon was like the one the cow jumped over in the nursery rhyme. She was a crescent, with a face in the hollow turned trustfully toward her husband the sun. The stars were their children, who seemed to run about the ceiling just as they pleased. The sun and the moon had regular motions, though, and rose and set at the proper times, for they were steady old folks.

The dream would always arrive in one way. I thought I awoke in the middle of the night, but there were the sun and the moon and the stars at their pranks and revels in the ceiling—Mr. Sun nodding and smiling to Mrs. Moon, and she nodding back to him with a knowing look and the corners of her mouth drawn down.

What I could hear of their talk seemed very odd indeed—about me, I fancied—but a thread of strong sense ran through it all. I would sometimes think of it the next day, and look up to the sun, thinking, *I wonder what he is seeing to talk to his wife about at night?* It sometimes made me a little more careful of my conduct.

In one corner of my dream ceiling there was a hole, and through that hole came down a ladder of bright and lovely sun rays—not from the sun, but from somewhere above and beyond the sun. I often tried to climb the ladder, but fast as I lifted my feet to climb, down they came again upon the boards of the floor.

We were four boys, but at the time the dreams were coming we had been five—there was a little baby brother, very ill, and not expected to live. I looked out from my bed one night and saw my mother bending over him in her lap. I fell asleep, but later woke and looked out again. Not only were my mother and the baby gone, but the cradle was too. I knew that my brother was dead. I did not cry: I was too young and ignorant to cry about it.

I went to sleep again, and woke into my dream. The sun and the moon were close together and talking very earnestly, and all the stars had gathered round them. I could not hear, but concluded they were talking about my little brother. *I suppose I ought to be sorry,* I said to myself—and I tried hard, but I could not feel sorry.

The heavenly host kept looking at me, and then at the corner where the ladder stood. I got out of bed and went to it, and to my delight found it would now bear me.

I climbed and climbed, and the sun and the moon and the stars looked more and more pleased as I drew nearer, till at last the sun smiled broadly. Then my head rose above them, and got out at the hole where the ladder came in. A wind blew upon me, a wind that I fancied was made of my baby brother's kisses. I began to love the little man who had lived only long enough to be our brother and get up above the sun and the moon and the stars by the ladder of sun rays. I began to weep for delight, and fell down the ladder into the room again and awoke, as one always does with a fall in a dream. Sun, moon, and stars were gone. The ladder of light had vanished, and I lay sobbing on my pillow.

The dream returned again and again, and it was not long after this that my mother died. I was sorrier for my father than for myself; he looked so sad. My mother was very good, and held my head to her chest as she was dying. I remember her death clearly; she was happy, and the least troubled of us all. Her sole concern was at leaving her husband and children, but the will of God was a better thing to her than to live with them. My sorrow at least was soon over, for God makes children so that grief cannot cleave to them.

When I see my mother again, she will not reproach me that my tears were so soon dried. "Little one," she may say, "how could you go on crying for your poor mother when God was mothering you all the time, and breathing life into you, and making the world a blessed place for you? You will tell me all about it some day."

Yes, and we shall tell our mothers how sorry we are that we ever gave them any trouble. Sometimes we were very naughty, and sometimes we did not know better.

CHAPTER TWO
My Father

My father was a tall, solemn man, who walked slowly with long strides. He spoke very little, and generally looked as if he were pondering next Sunday's sermon. His head was gray, and a little bent, as if he were gathering truth from the ground. Once I came upon him in the garden, standing with his face up to heaven, and I thought he was seeing something in the clouds. But then I saw that his eyes were closed, and I crept away as if I had been peeping where I should not be.

After my mother's death he did not talk much to us, but what he said was very gentle. He used to walk much about his fields, especially on summer mornings before the sun was up. I presume he felt nearer to her in the fields than in the house.

I never had the least doubt that my father was the best man in the world. I am still of the same opinion, though the son of the village tailor once gave me a tremendous thrashing for saying so. He told me that I was altogether wrong, for *his* father was the best man in the world. I modified the assertion only to this extent: that my father was the best man *I* have ever known.

There was a kind of grandeur about him, and we feared and loved him both at once. I do not remember ever being punished by him, but I have been told that he did punish us when we were very small. And I cannot say that I learned much from his sermons. Though I loved the sound of his voice, and liked to look at his face as he stood in the ancient pulpit, I never cared much about what he said. Of course it was a better sermon than any other clergyman could have preached, but its subject was of no consequence to me.

The church, a very old one with a short square tower, seemed to be settling down again into the earth, especially on one side where great buttresses had been built to keep it up. It leaned against them like a weary old thing that wanted to go to sleep. Though there was but one old cracked bell in its tower, though there was no organ to give out its glorious sounds, though there was neither chanting nor responses, the awe and reverence which fell upon me there were immense. There was a hush in it which demanded a refraining of the foot, a treading softly as upon holy ground; and the church was inseparably associated with my father.

The pew we sat in was square, giving us each a corner, with a table in the middle of it for our books. David generally used it for laying his head upon, that he might go to sleep comfortably. Tom put his feet on the crossbar, leaned back in his corner, put his hands in his trousers pockets, and stared hard at my father. Allister, whose back was to the pulpit, used to learn the paraphrases* during the sermon. I, happiest of all in my position, could look up at my father, if I pleased, a little sideways; or, if I preferred, which I often did, study the figure of an armed knight, carved in stone, which lay on the top of the tomb of Sir Worm Wymble. The tomb was close by our pew, with only a flagged passage between. It stood in a hollow in the wall, and the knight lay under the arch of the recess, so silent, so patient, with folded palms, as if praying for help. Organ and chant were not altogether needful while the carved knight lay there with his face upturned to heaven.

But from gazing at the knight I began to regard the wall about him, and the arch over him. Then my eye would seek the roof and descend to the pillars, or wander about the

---

*You can find an explanation of the starred words in the Glossary, pages 166-167.

windows, discovering the strength of the place and how it was upheld. So while my father was talking of the church as a company of believers, and describing how it was held together by faith, I was trying to understand how the stone and lime of the old place was kept from falling apart. Thus I began my profession: I am an architect.

My father always spoke in a low, earnest voice, and every eye but mine and those of two of my brothers was fixed upon him. And even Tom, with all his staring, knew as little about the sermon as any of us. But my father did not question us much concerning it; he did what was far better.

On Sunday afternoons, in the warm, peaceful sunlight of summer, with the honeysuckle filling the air of the little arbor in which we sat, our father would sit for an hour talking away to us in his gentle, slow, deep voice, telling us story after story out of the New Testament, and explaining them in a way I have seldom heard equalled.

Or, in the cold winter nights, he would come into the room where I and my two younger brothers slept and, sitting down with Tom by his side before the fire that burned bright in the frosty air. My father would open the great family Bible on the table, turn his face toward the two beds where we three lay wide awake, and tell us story after story out of the Old Testament, turning the bare facts into an expanded and illustrated narrative of his own. I shall never forget Joseph in Egypt hearing the pattering of the asses' hooves in the street, and throwing up the window, and looking out, and seeing all his own brothers coming riding toward him; or the grand rush of the sea waves over the bewildered Egyptians.

We lay and listened with all the more enjoyment, that while the fire was burning so brightly, and the presence of my father was filling the room with safety and peace, the wind was howling outside, and the snow was drifting up against the window. Sometimes I passed into the land of sleep with his voice in my ears and his love in my heart.

CHAPTER THREE

Mrs. Mitchell and Kirsty

My father had a housekeeper, Mrs. Mitchell—a trusty woman, as he considered her. We thought she was very old, though I suppose she was about 40. She was not pleasant, but grim-faced and disapproving, with a very straight back and a very long upper lip.

She was always making some complaint to my father against us. Perhaps she meant to speak the truth, or took it for granted that she always *did* speak the truth. But she would exaggerate things, and give them quite another look. The bones of her story might be true, but she would put a skin over it after her own fashion, which was not one of mildness and charity. So the older we grew, the more our minds were alienated from her, and the more we regarded her as our enemy. If she really meant to be our friend, it was at least an uncomely kind of friendship, showing itself in constant opposition, fault-finding, and complaint.

Our real mistake was that we were boys. There was something in Mrs. Mitchell that was opposed to the nature of boys. You would have thought that to be a boy was in her eyes to be something wrong to begin with—that boys ought never to have been made, and that they must always, by their very nature, be doing something amiss. My father would hear her complaints without putting in a word, except to ask her a question. When she had finished, he would turn again to his book or his sermon, saying, "Very well, Mrs. Mitchell. I will speak to them about it."

He apparently did not believe much of what she told him. At all events, when he had sent for us, he would ask our version of the affair, and listen to that as he had listened to hers. Then he would explain to us where we had been wrong, if we were wrong, and send us away with a warning not to provoke Mrs. Mitchell, who couldn't help being short in her temper!

She was saving even to stinginess. She would do her best to provide what my father liked, but for us she thought almost anything good enough. She would give us the thinnest of milk—we said she skimmed it three times before she thought it blue enough for us.

In contrast, Kirsty was a Highland woman who had the charge of the house in which the farm servants lived. She was a cheerful, gracious, kind woman—a woman of God's making, though we cannot deny that He made Mrs. Mitchell too. Once my brother Davie came running in great distress to Kirsty, crying, "Fee, fee!" which meant that a flea was making his life miserable. Kirsty undressed him and entered on the pursuit. After a successful search, little Davie, who had been looking very solemn and thoughtful, concluded, "God didn't make the fees, Kirsty!"

"Oh yes, Davie! God made everything. God *did* make the fleas," Kirsty said.

Davie was silent for a while. Then he opened his mouth and spoke like a discontented prophet of old, "Why doesn't He give them something else to eat, then?"

"You must ask Him that," said Kirsty, with a wisdom I have since learned to comprehend, though it shocked me at the time.

All this set me thinking, and I put my own question to Kirsty. "Then I suppose God made Mrs. Mitchell as well as you and the rest of us, Kirsty?"

"Certainly, Ranald," returned Kirsty.

"Well, I wish He hadn't," I remarked.

"Oh! She's not a bad sort," said Kirsty, "though if I were her, I would try to be a little more agreeable."

Kirsty was our constant resort. The farmhouse was a furlong* or so from the manse, but with the blood pouring from a cut finger, we would run that furlong rather than go to Mrs. Mitchell for help. Kirsty was dear, and good, and kind, our refuge in all time of trouble and necessity. It was she who gave us something to eat as we wanted, for she said it was no cheating of the minister to feed the minister's boys.

Kirsty was short and slender, with keen blue eyes and dark hair; an uncommonly small foot, which she claimed for all Highland folk; a light step, a sweet voice, and a most bounteous hand. Her face was the sign of good to me and my brothers; I loved her so much that I do not know now, even as I did not care then, whether she was nice-looking or not. Kirsty was quite as old as Mrs. Mitchell, but we never thought of her being old.

And then her stories! There was nothing like them in all that countryside. It was rather a dreary country, having many bleak moorland hills, that lay about like slow-stiffened waves, of no great height but of much desolation. As far as the imagination was concerned, it would seem that the minds of former generations had been as bleak as the country, they had left such small store of legends of any sort.

But Kirsty had come from a region where the hills were hills indeed—hills with mighty skeletons of stone inside them; hills that looked as if they had been heaped over huge monsters which were ever trying to get up—a country where every cliff and rock and well had its story. After supper we would sit by her fire, and Kirsty would tell us stories, and we were in our heaven.

CHAPTER FOUR
I Begin "Life"

I began "life"—after no pleasant fashion—when I was about six. One glorious morning in early summer I found myself half-dragged by Mrs. Mitchell's ungentle hand toward a little school on the outside of the village. I looked around at the shining fields and up at the blue sky with the despair of a man going to the gallows and bidding farewell to the world. It was very bitter, especially as a lark was singing, and there was the loveliest sunshine, and I had expected to go with my elder brother to spend the day at a neighboring farm.

We had to cross a little stream, and in the middle of the footbridge I tugged again at my imprisoned hand, with a half-formed intention of throwing myself into the brook. But my efforts were still unavailing. Over a half-mile or so I was led to the cottage door—not a cottage with roses and honeysuckle hiding its walls, but a dreary little house with nothing green to cover its brown stones.

Mrs. Mitchell opened the door and led me in. Dame Shand, the teacher, stood at her table ironing. She was as tall as Mrs. Mitchell, and that turned me against her at once. She wore a close-fitting widow's cap with a black ribbon round it. Her hair was grey, and her face was as grey as her hair, and her skin was gathered in wrinkles about her mouth, where they twitched and twitched, as if she were constantly meditating something unpleasant. She looked up inquiringly.

"I've brought you a new scholar," Mrs. Mitchell said.

"Very well," said Dame Shand, in a dubious tone. "I hope he's a good boy, for he must be good if he comes here."

"Well, he's just middling. His father spares the rod, Mrs. Shand, and we *know* what comes of that."

They went on with their talk, which was complimentary to none but themselves. Meanwhile, I was making what observations my terror would allow. About a dozen children were seated on benches along the walls, looking at me over the tops of their spelling books. In the far corner two were kicking at each other as opportunity offered, looking very angry, but not daring to cry. My next discovery was terribly disconcerting: I saw a boy of my own age on the floor, fastened by a string to a leg of the ironing table. And an ugly dog, big enough to be frightened at, lay under the table, watching the boy. I gazed in utter dismay.

"Ah, you may look!" said the dame. "If you're not a good boy, that is how you shall be treated. The dog shall have you to look after."

I trembled, and was speechless. After some further confabulation, Mrs. Mitchell took her leave, saying, "I'll come back for him at one o'clock, and if I don't come, just keep him till I do come."

The dame accompanied Mrs. Mitchell to the door, and then I discovered that she was lame, and hobbled very much. An idea arose full-formed in my brain.

I sat down on the form* near the door, and kept very quiet. When Dame Shand returned, she resumed her ironing, then called me to her by name. I obeyed, trembling.

"Can you say your letters?" she asked.

Although I could not read, I could repeat the alphabet, and did so.

"How many questions of your catechism* can you say?" she asked next.

Not knowing with certainty what she meant, I was silent.

"No sulking!" said the dame, and opening a drawer in the table, she took out a catechism. Turning back the cover she put it in my hand, and told me to learn the first question. She had not even asked whether I could read. I took the catechism, and stood as before.

"Go to your seat," she said.

I obeyed, and with the book before me pondered my plan. Everything depended on whether I could open the door before she could reach me. Once out of the house, I was sure of running faster than she could follow.

The ironing required a fire to make the irons hot. As the morning went on, the sunshine on the walls, conspiring with the fire on the hearth, made the place too hot for the dame's comfort. She went and set the door wide open. I was instantly on the alert, watching for an opportunity, and one soon occurred.

A class of some five or six was reading, if reading it could be called, out of the Bible. At length it came to the turn of one who blundered dreadfully—the same boy who had been tied under the table, and released for his lesson. The dame hobbled to him, and found he had his book upside down, whereupon she turned in wrath to the table, and took from the drawer a long leather strap, with which she proceeded to chastise him. As his first cry reached my ears, I was halfway to the door.

"The new boy's running away!" shrieked some little tattle-tale inside.

I had not gone many yards from the cottage before I heard her voice screaming after me to return. I took no heed—only sped the faster. But her command was enforced by the paralyzing bark of her pursuing prime minister! I turned, and there was the fiendish dog close on my heels.

For one moment I felt as if I should sink to the earth for sheer terror, but the next moment a wholesome rage sent the blood to my brain. I rushed toward the little wretch, threw myself upon him in desperation, and dug my nails into him. The coward yelped and howled, struggled from my grasp, and ran with his tail merged in his person back to his mistress, who was hobbling after me. But with the renewed strength of triumph I turned again and ran for home. I never turned my head until I laid it on Kirsty's bosom, sobbing and crying.

As soon as Kirsty succeeded in calming me, I told her the whole story. She said very little, but I could see she was very angry. No doubt she was pondering what could be done. She got me some milk—half cream I do believe—and some oatcake, and went on with her work.

I thought that any moment Mrs. Mitchell might appear to drag me back to that horrible den. I knew that Kirsty's authority was not equal to hers, and that she would be compelled to give me up. So I watched an opportunity to escape once more and hide myself, so that even Kirsty might be able to say she did not know where I was.

When I had finished, and Kirsty had left the kitchen, I sped noiselessly to the door, and looked out into the empty farmyard. Dark and brown and cool the door of the barn stood open, inviting me to shelter and safety. I sped across the sunshine into the darkness, and began burrowing in a great heap of straw like a wild animal. I drew out handfuls of straw and laid them carefully aside, so that no disorder should betray my retreat. When I had made a hole large enough to hold me, I got in, but kept drawing out the straw behind me, and filling the hole in front. This I continued until I had not only stopped up the entrance, but placed a good thickness of straw between me and the outside. By the time I had burrowed as far as I thought necessary, I was tired, and lay down delighting in safety. I was soon fast asleep.

CHAPTER FIVE
No Father

I awoke, crept out of my lair, peeped from the door of the barn into the corn yard, and found that the sun was going down. I had already discovered that I was getting hungry. I went out at the other door into the farmyard, and ran across to the house. No one was there. But, to my dismay, I saw Mrs. Mitchell coming toward the farm. I ran first to Kirsty's press* and secured a good supply of oatcake, and then sped like a hunted hare to my hole. I began to eat, and fell asleep again before I had finished.

As I slept I dreamed my dream again—that the sun was looking very grave, and the moon reflected his concern. They were not satisfied with me. At length the sun shook his head—that is, his whole self—and the moon shook herself in response. Then they began to talk, both at once, yet each listening while each spoke. I heard no words, but their lips moved busily, their eyebrows went up and down, and their eyelids winked. There was a storm of expression upon their faces; their very noses twisted and curled. The stars darted about, gathered into groups, dispersed, and formed new groups. Some of them kept darting up and down the ladder of rays, like phosphorescent sparks in the sea foam.

I could bear it no longer, and awoke. I was in darkness, but not in my own bed. When I tried to turn, I found myself hemmed in on all sides. I could not stretch my arms, and there was hardly room for my body between my feet and my head. I was dreadfully frightened at first, and felt as if I were being slowly stifled. But then my brain awoke, and I recalled the horrible events of the day.

I drew away the straw from the entrance to my lair, but even when my hand went out into space no light came through the opening. I shot out the remainder of the stopper of straw, and crept from the hole. In the great barn there was but the dullest glimmer of light. I tumbled through one of the doors into the dark night. Before me was the corn yard, full of ricks.* Between their tops I saw only stars and darkness.

I stepped out into the night with the grass of the corn yard under my feet, the awful vault of heaven over my head, and those shadowy ricks around me. I groped my way through them, and got out into the open field by creeping between the stems of what had once been a hawthorn hedge, but had in the course of a hundred years grown into a grim, large, grotesque tree.

I stood in the vast hall of the silent night—alone: there lay the awfulness of it. I had never before known what the night was. The real sting of its fear lay in this—that there was nobody else in it. Everybody but me was asleep all over the world, and had abandoned me to my fate.

When I rounded the edge of the stone wall, which on another side bounded the corn yard, there was the crescent moon, as I saw her in my dream, but low down toward the horizon, and lying almost upon her rounded back. She looked very disconsolate and dim. Even she would take no heed of me, abandoned child! The stars were high up, away in the heavens. They did not look like the children of the sun and moon at all, and they took no heed of me. Yet there was a grandeur in my desolation that would have elevated my heart but for the fear. It was not dark out here in the open field, for at this season of the year it is not dark there all night long, when the sky is unclouded. Away in the north was the Great Bear by which one of the men had taught me to find the North Star. Nearly under it was the light of the sun, creeping round by the north toward the spot in the east where he would rise again.

I gazed at that pale faded light, and all at once I remembered that God was near me. But I did not know who God was then as I know now, and when I thought about Him then, my idea of Him was not like Him; it was merely a confused mixture of other people's fancies about Him as well as my own. I had not learned how beautiful God is; I had only learned that He is strong. I had been told that He was angry with those who did wrong; I had not understood that He loved them all the time, though He was displeased with them, and must punish them to make them good. When I thought of Him now in the silent starry night, great terror seized me, and I stumbled over the uneven field.

Where should I fly but home? True, Mrs. Mitchell was there, but there was another there as well. Even Kirsty would not do in this terror. Home was the only refuge, for my father was there. I sped for the manse.

I approached it, and stood on the grass-plot in front of the house. There was no light in its eyes, and its mouth was closed. Above it shone the speechless stars. Nothing was alive. Nothing would speak. I went up the few rough-hewn granite steps, laid my hand on the handle, and gently turned it. The door opened, and I entered the hall, but no footsteps echoed, and no voices were there. I closed the door behind me, and, almost sick with the misery of a being where no other being was to comfort it, I groped my way to my father's room. When I once had my hand on his door, the warm tide of courage began again to flow from my heart. I opened this door too very quietly, for was not the dragon asleep down below?

"Papa! Papa!" I whispered eagerly. "Are you awake?"

No voice came in reply, and the place was yet more silent than the night or the hall. He must be asleep.

I was afraid to call louder. I crept nearer to the bed, and stretched out my hands to feel for him. He must be at the farther side. I climbed up on the bed, and felt all across it. Utter desertion seized my soul—my father was not there! My heart sank totally within me. I fell down on the bed weeping bitterly, and wept myself asleep.

(Years after, when I was a young man, I read of another man's terrible dream that there was no God. The desolation of this night was my key to understanding that dream.)

Once more I awoke to a sense of misery, and stretched out my arms, crying, "Papa! Papa!"

The same moment I found my father's arms around me; he folded me close to him, and said, "Hush, Ranald, my boy! Here I am! You are quite safe."

I nestled as close to him as I could go, and wept for blessedness. "O Papa!" I sobbed. "I thought I had lost you."

"And I thought I had lost you, my boy. Tell me all about it."

He had soon gathered the whole story, and I in my turn learned the dismay of the household when I did not appear. Kirsty had told what she knew. They searched everywhere, but could not find me. As great as my misery had been, my father's had been greater than mine. While I stood forsaken and desolate in the field, they had been searching along the riverbanks. But the herdsman had had an idea, and although they had already searched the barn and every place they could think of, he left them and ran back for a further search about the farm. Guided by the scattered straw, he soon came upon my deserted lair, and sped back to the riverside with the news. When my father returned, and failed to find me in my own bed, to his infinite relief he found me fast asleep on his. I had already slept so long, but sorrow is very sleepy.

CHAPTER SIX

Mrs. Mitchell Is Defeated

After this talk with my father I fell into a sleep of perfect contentment, and never thought of what might be on the morrow till the morrow came. Then I realized I was in danger of being carried off once more to school unless my father interfered. I thought he would protect me, but I had no assurance. I got up at once, intending to find him—but, to my horror, before I was half-dressed, Mrs. Mitchell came into the room, looking triumphant and revengeful.

"I'm glad to see you're getting up," she said, her eyes fierce with suppressed indignation. "It's nearly *school* time."

"I haven't had my porridge," I said.

"Your porridge is waiting you—as cold as a stone," she answered. "If boys will lie in bed so late, what can they expect?"

"Nothing from you," I muttered.

"What's that you're saying?" she asked angrily.

I was silent.

"Don't keep me waiting all day," she said.

"You needn't wait, Mrs. Mitchell. I am dressing as fast as I can. Is Papa in his study yet?"

"No. And you needn't think to see him. He's angry enough with you, I dare say." She had no idea what had passed between my father and me already. She could not imagine what a talk we had had.

"You needn't think to run away as you did yesterday," she continued. "Mrs. Shand told me all about it. I shouldn't wonder if your papa's gone to see her now, and tell her how sorry he is you were so naughty."

"I'm *not* going to school till I've seen Papa. If he says I'm to go, I will, of course—but I won't go for you."

"You will, and you won't!" she repeated, standing staring at me. "That's all very fine, but I know something a good deal finer. Now wash your face."

"I won't, so long as you stand there," I said, and sat down on the floor. She advanced toward me.

"If you touch me, I'll scream!" I cried.

She stopped, thought for a moment, and bounced out of the room. But I heard her turn the key of the door.

I dressed as fast as I could, then opened the window, which was only a few feet from the ground, scrambled out, and dropped. I fled for the harbor of Kirsty's arms, but as I turned the corner of the house I ran right into Mrs. Mitchell, who received me with no soft embrace. In fact I was rather severely scratched with a pin on the front of her dress.

"There! That serves you right!" she cried. "That's a judgment on you for trying to run away again. You are a bad boy!"

"Why am I a bad boy?" I retorted.

"It's bad not to do what you are told."

"I will do what my papa tells me."

"Your papa! There are more people than your papa in the world."

"I'm a bad boy if I don't do what anybody like you chooses to tell me, am I?"

"None of your impudence!" This was accompanied by a box on the ear as she dragged me into the kitchen. There she set my porridge before me, which I declined to eat.

"Well, if you won't eat good food, you shall go to school without it."

"I tell you I won't go to school!"

She caught me up in her strong arms, and I could not prevent her from carrying me out of the house. If I had been the bad boy she said I was, I could by biting and scratching have made her set me down; but I felt that I must not do that, for then I should be ashamed before my father. Therefore I yielded for the time, but I drew the pin from her dress; if she did not set me down soon, I would make her glad to do so. When we came to the footbridge, which had but one rail to it, I would stick the pin into her and make her let me go. Then I would throw myself into the river, for I would run the risk of being drowned rather than go to that school. Were all my griefs of yesterday, overcome and on the point of being forgotten, to be frustrated in this fashion? I was convinced my father did not want me to go. He could not have been so kind to me during the night, and then send me to such a place in the morning.

Before we were out of the gate, I heard my father calling Mrs. Mitchell. Seeing him coming after us with his long strides, I struggled violently in the strength of hope, broke away, ran to my father, and burst out crying.

"Papa! Papa!" I sobbed. "Don't send me to that horrid school! I can learn to read without that old woman to teach me."

"Really, Mrs. Mitchell," said my father, taking me by the hand and leading me toward her, where she stood visibly flaming with rage and annoyance. "You are taking too much upon yourself! I never said that Ranald was to go to that woman's school. In fact, I don't approve of what I hear of her, and I have thought of consulting some of my brethren in the presbytery on the matter before taking steps myself. I won't have the young people in my parish oppressed in such a fashion. Terrified with dogs too! It is shameful."

"She's a very decent woman, is Mistress Shand," said the housekeeper.

"I don't dispute her decency, Mrs. Mitchell, but I doubt very much whether she is fit to have the charge of children. And, as she is a friend of yours, you will be doing her a kindness to give her a hint to that effect. It may save the necessity for my taking further and more unpleasant steps."

"Indeed, sir, by your leave, it would be hard to take the bread out of the mouth of a lone widow woman, and bring her upon the parish with a bad name to boot. She's supported herself for years with her school, and been a trouble to nobody."

"Except the lambs of the flock, Mrs. Mitchell," my father replied. "I like you for standing up for your friend. But is a woman, because she is lone and a widow, to make a Moloch* of herself, and have the children sacrificed to her in that way? It's enough to make idiots of some of them. She had better see to it. You tell her that—from me, if you like. I'll take my young men," he added with a smile, "to school when I see fit."

"I'm sure, sir," said Mrs. Mitchell, putting her blue striped apron to her eyes, "I asked your opinion before I took him."

"I believe I did say something about it being time Ranald were able to read, but nothing more. You must have misunderstood me," he added, willing to ease her descent to the valley of her humiliation.

Mrs. Mitchell walked away without another word, sniffing the air as she went, and carrying her hands folded under her apron. From that hour, I believe she hated me.

My father looked after her with a smile, and then looked down on me, saying, "She's short in the temper, poor woman! We mustn't provoke her."

I was too well satisfied to urge my victory by further complaint. I had been delivered as from the fiery furnace, and the earth and the sky were laughing around me. Oh! What a sunshine filled the world! How glad were the larks that blessed morning! The demon of oppression had hidden her head ashamed, and fled to her den!

CHAPTER SEVEN
A New Schoolmistress

"But, Ranald," my father continued, "what are we to do about the reading? I didn't want to make learning a burden to you, and I don't approve of children learning to read too soon. But it is time you were beginning. I have time to teach you some things, but I can't teach you everything. I have to read a great deal, and think a great deal, and go about my parish a good deal. And your brother Tom has heavy lessons to learn at school, and I have to help him. So what's to be done, Ranald, my boy? You can't go to the parish school before you've learned your letters."

"There's Kirsty, Papa," I suggested.

"Kirsty can do everything, can't she?"

"She can speak Gaelic,*" I said with a tone of triumph.

"I wish you could speak Gaelic," said my father, thinking of his wife, I believe, whose mother tongue it was. "But that is not what you want most to learn. Do you think Kirsty could teach you to read English?"

"Yes, I do."

"Let us go and ask her," he said, taking my hand.

I capered with delight, nor ceased my capering till we stood on Kirsty's earthen floor. She was dusting one of her deal* chairs, as white as soap and sand could make it, for the minister to sit on. She was a great favorite with my father, and he always behaved as a visitor in her house.

"Well, Kirsty," he said, after the first greetings were over, "have you any objection to turn schoolmistress?"

"I should make a poor hand at that," she answered, with a smile to me which showed she guessed what my father

30

wanted. "But if it were to teach Master Ranald there, I should like dearly to try what I could do."

Had Kirsty's speech been in the coarse dialect of Mrs. Mitchell, I am confident my father would not have allowed her to teach me. But Kirsty did not speak a word of Scotch, and although her English was a little broken and odd, being formed somewhat after Gaelic idioms, her tone was pure and her phrases were refined.

Kirsty had come to the manse with my mother, and my father was attached to her for the sake of his wife as well as for her own, and Kirsty would have died for the minister or any one of his boys. All the devotion a Highland woman has for the chief of her clan, Kirsty had for my father, plus the reverence due to the minister.

After a little chat, my father rose, saying, "Then I'll just turn Ranald over to you, Kirsty. Do you think you can manage without letting it interfere with your work, though?"

"Oh yes, sir! I shall soon have him reading to me while I'm busy about. If he doesn't know the word, he can spell it, and then I shall know it—at least, if it's not longer than Hawkie's tail."

Hawkie was a fine milk cow, with a bad temper and a comically short tail. It had been chopped off in an accident when she was a calf.

"There's something else short about Hawkie—isn't there, Kirsty?" said my father.

"And Mrs. Mitchell," I suggested, thinking to help Kirsty to my father's meaning.

"Come, come, young gentleman! We don't want your remarks," said my father pleasantly.

"Why, Papa, you told me so yourself, just before we came up."

"Yes, I did—but I did not mean you to repeat it. What if Kirsty were to go and tell Mrs. Mitchell?"

Kirsty knew well enough that my father knew there was no danger. She only laughed, and I, seeing Kirsty satisfied, was satisfied also, and joined in the laugh.

* * * * *

Before many weeks had passed, Allister and wee Davie were Kirsty's pupils also. Allister was learning to read, and wee Davie was learning to sit still, which was the hardest task within his capacity. They were free to come or keep away, but not to go: if they did come, Kirsty insisted on their staying out the lesson.

So every morning in summer we might be seen perched on a form, under one of the tiny windows, in that delicious brown light which you seldom find but in an old clay-floored cottage. In the winter, we seated ourselves as near the fire as Kirsty's cooking operations admitted. It was delightful to us boys, and would have been amusing to anyone, to see how Kirsty behaved when Mrs. Mitchell found occasion to pay a visit during lesson hours. Kirsty knew the woman's footsteps and always darted to the door; not once did she permit Mrs. Mitchell to enter.

"No, you'll not come in just now, Mrs. Mitchell," she would say, as the housekeeper attempted to pass. "You know we're busy."

"I want to hear how they're getting on."

"You can try them at home," Kirsty would answer. We always laughed at the idea of our reading to Mrs. Mitchell. Once I believe she heard the laugh, for she instantly walked away, and I do not remember that she ever came again.

CHAPTER EIGHT

We Learn Other Things

We boys were more than ever at the farm now. During the summer, from the time we got up till the time we went to bed, we seldom approached the manse. I have heard it hinted that my father neglected us. But that can hardly be, seeing that then his word was law to us, and now I regard his memory as the symbol of the love unspeakable.

My father did not mind his younger sons running wild; Kirsty was there for them to run to, and the men were careful over us as well. No doubt we were rather savage, very different in our appearance from town-bred children, who were washed and dressed every time they went out for a walk: *that* we should have considered not merely a hardship, but an indignity. To be free was our notion of a perfect existence. But my father's rebuke was awful indeed, if he found even the youngest son guilty of untruth, or cruelty, or injustice. At all kinds of escapades, not involving disobedience, he smiled, except indeed there were too much danger, when he would warn and limit.

Almost everything was an amusement. Our farm was not at all like some great farm in England; there was nothing done by machinery on our place. If there had been a steam engine to plow my father's fields, how could we have ridden home on its back in the evening? To ride the horses home after plowing was a triumph. Had there been a threshing-machine, could its pleasures have been comparable to that of lying in the straw and watching the grain dance from the sheaves under the skillful flails of the two strong men who belabored them?

I could drive the wheel of the winnowing machine myself, and watch the storm of chaff driven like snowflakes from its wide mouth. While the grain was flowing in a silent slow stream from the shelving hole into the other side, the wind that rushed through the door caught the expelled chaff and carried it farther away.

Eppie, a beggar woman, would come and fill her sack with what the wind blew her. She did not covet the grain; she only wanted her bed filled with fresh springy chaff, on which she would sleep as sound as her rheumatism would let her, and as warm and dry as any duchess in the land.

We were allowed to take the workhorses at watering-time from the stable to the long trough that stood under the pump. There they would drop head and neck and shoulders, causing us a vague fear of falling over forward. They would drink and drink till our legs felt their bodies swelling under us. Then up and away they would go with refreshed stride toward the paradise of their stalls.

But first came the fearful pass of the stable door. The horses never stopped at the stable door to let their riders dismount, but walked right in. There was just room, by stooping low, to clear the top of the door. As we improved in horsemanship, we would go afield to ride them home from the pasture. There was more adventure here, for not only was the ride longer, but the horses were more frisky, and would sometimes set off at a gallop. Then the chief danger was again the door, lest they should dash in, and knock our knees against the posts and our heads against the lintels, for we had only halters to hold them with. But after I had once been thrown during a wild gallop, I was raised to the dignity of a bridle.

It was my father's express desire that until we could sit well bareback we should not be allowed a saddle. It was a whole year before I was permitted to mount Missy, his little black riding mare. She was old, it is true—nobody quite knew how old—but if she felt a light weight on her back, she would dart off like the wind. Yet in after years I would climb upon her back, and lie there reading my book, while she mashed away at the grass as if nobody were near her.

And we could always go to the field where the cattle were grazing. How we loved the rich hot summer afternoons among the grass and the clover, the little lamb-daisies, and the big horse-daisies! And there was pleasure in the company and devices of the cowherd, a freckle-faced, white-haired, weak-eyed boy of ten. We called him *Turkey,* because his nose was the color of a turkey's egg. Who but Turkey knew mushrooms from toadstools? Who but Turkey knew the note and the form and the nest and the eggs of every bird in the country? Who but Turkey, with his little whip and its lash of brass wire, would encounter the angriest bull in Christendom? Who like Turkey could rob a wild bee's nest? And who could be more just than he in distributing the luscious prize? His accomplishments were innumerable. Short of flying, we believed him capable of anything.

He was also dear to us because there was enmity between him and Mrs. Mitchell. It came about in this way. Although a good milker, and therefore a good feeder, Hawkie was yet tempted to an unnatural appetite. When Hawkie found a piece of an old shoe in the field, she would, if not compelled to drop the delicious mouthful, go on chewing the impossible but savoury morsel. Should this happen, Turkey's inattention could not escape discovery; the milkpail would soon reveal the fact to Kirsty's watchful eyes.

But Hawkie's morbid craving was not confined to old shoes. One day when the cattle were feeding close by the manse, she found Mrs. Mitchell's best cap on the holly hedge, laid out to bleach in the sun. It was a tempting morsel—easier to chew than shoe-leather. Mrs. Mitchell returned only in time to see one long string gradually disappearing into Hawkie's mouth. With a wild cry of despair she flew at Hawkie, laid hold of the string, and drew the deplorable mass from her throat. And Turkey, who had come running at Mrs. Mitchell's cry, received the slimy and sloppy remains full in his face. Then Mrs. Mitchell flew at him in her fury, and with an outburst of abuse boxed his ears soundly, before he could recover his senses sufficiently to run away. Thus Turkey became her enemy, before he knew that we also had good grounds for disliking her.

And Turkey was as fond of Kirsty's stories as we were. In the winter especially we would sit together in the evening, as I have already said, around her fire and the great pot upon it full of the most delicious potatoes. Kirsty knitted away vigorously at her blue broad-ribbed stockings, and kept a sort of time to her story with the sound of her needles. When the story flagged, the needles went slower, while in the more animated passages they would become invisible for swiftness, save for a certain shimmering flash that hovered about her fingers. But when they ceased altogether, we knew that some awful crisis indeed was at hand.

CHAPTER NINE

Sir Worm Wymble

It was a snowy evening in the depth of winter. Kirsty had promised to tell us the tale of the armed knight who lay in stone upon the tomb in the church; but the snow was so deep that Mrs. Mitchell, always glad when nature put it in her power to exercise her authority in a way disagreeable to us, had refused to let the little ones go out all day. Therefore, when the darkness began to grow thick enough, Turkey and I went prowling and watching about the manse until Mrs. Mitchell was out of the way. Then we darted into the nursery, caught up my two brothers, hoisted them on our backs, and rushed from the house.

The snow was coming down in huge flakes, but though it was only half-past four o'clock, they did not show any whiteness, for there was no light to shine upon them. How the little ones did enjoy it, spurring their horses with suppressed laughter, and urging us on lest the old witch should hear and overtake us! "Doe on, doe on, Yanal!" cried Davie, and "Yanal" did his very best, but was only halfway through the deep snow to the farm when Turkey came bounding back to take Davie from him. In a few moments we had shaken the snow off our shoes and off Davie's back, and stood around Kirsty's "booful baze," as Davie called the fire. Kirsty seated herself on one side with Davie on her lap, and we three got our chairs as near her as we could, with the valiant Turkey farthest from the center of safety, namely Kirsty, who was at the same time to be the source of all the delightful horror.

"There is a pot in the Highlands," began Kirsty, "not far

37

from our house, at the bottom of a little glen. It is not very big, but they do say there is no bottom to it."

"An iron pot, Kirsty?" asked Allister.

"No, goosey," answered Kirsty. "A pot means a great hole full of water—black and deep."

"Oh!" remarked Allister, and was silent.

"Well, in this pot there lived a kelpie."

"What's a kelpie, Kirsty?" again interposed Allister.

"A kelpie is an awful creature that eats people. It's something like a horse, with a head like a cow, but bigger than Hawkie—bigger than the biggest ox you ever saw."

"Has it a great mouth?"

"Yes, a terrible mouth."

"With teeth?"

"Not many, but dreadfully big ones."

"Oh!"

"Well, there was a shepherd many years ago, who lived not far from the pot. He was a knowing man, and understood all about kelpies and brownies and fairies. And he put a branch of the rowan tree with the red berries in it over the door of his cottage so that the kelpie could never come in.

"The shepherd had a very beautiful daughter, and the kelpie wanted very much to eat her. I suppose he had lifted up his head out of the pot one day and seen her go past, but he could not come out of the pot except after the sun was down. His eyes couldn't bear the light, but he could see in the dark quite well.

"One night the girl woke suddenly, and saw the kelpie looking in at her window, but he couldn't get in. He was thinking how he should like to eat her. So in the morning she told her father. He was very frightened, and told her she must *never* be out one moment after the sun was down.

"For a long time the girl was very careful. But one afternoon she had gone to meet her lover a little way down the glen, and they talked so long that the sun was almost set before she realized it. She said good-night at once, and ran for home.

"Now she could not reach home without passing the pot, and just as she passed it, she saw the last sparkle of the sun as he went down. And behind her she heard a great *whish* of water tumbling off the beast's back as he came up from the bottom. If she ran before, she *flew* now. And the worst of it was that she couldn't hear him behind her, and he might be just opening his mouth to take her any moment! At last she reached the door, which her father, who had gone out looking for her, had set wide open so she might run in at once—but all the breath was out of her body, and she fell down flat just as she got inside."

Here Allister jumped from his seat, clapping his hands and crying, "The kelpie didn't eat her! Kirsty!"

"No, but as she fell, one foot was left outside the door, so that the rowan branch could not take care of it. And the beast laid hold of her foot, to drag her out of the cottage and eat her. But her shoe came off in his mouth, and she drew in her foot and was safe."

Allister drew a deep breath, and sat down again.

But Turkey broke in with, "I don't believe a word of it, Kirsty."

"What!" said Kirsty. "You don't believe it?"

"No. She lost her shoe in the mud. It was some wild duck she heard in the pot, and there was no beast after her. She never saw it, you know."

"She saw it look in at her window."

"Yes, yes. That was in the middle of the night. I've seen as much myself when I waked up in the middle of the night. I took a rat for a tiger once."

Kirsty was looking angry, and her knitting needles were going even faster than when she reached the climax of the shoe.

"Hold your tongue, Turkey," I said, "and let us hear the rest of the story."

But Kirsty kept her eyes on her knitting, and did not resume.

"Is that all, Kirsty?" asked Allister.

Still Kirsty returned no answer. She needed all her force to overcome the anger she was busy stifling. For it would never do for one in her position to lose her temper because of the unbelieving criticism of a herd-boy. After a few moments she began again as if she had never stopped and no remarks had been made, only her voice trembled a little at first.

"Her father came home soon after, in great distress, and found her lying just within the door. His anger was kindled against her lover more than the beast, although he was a gentleman and his daughter only a shepherd's daughter. And they were both of the blood of the MacLeods."

This was Kirsty's own clan.

"But why was he angry with the gentleman?" asked Allister.

"Because the gentleman liked her company better than he loved herself," said Kirsty. "The shepherd said the young man ought to have seen her safely home. But he didn't know then that MacLeod's own father had threatened to kill the young man if ever he spoke to the girl again."

"But," said Allister, "I thought the story was about Sir Worm Wymble—not Mr. MacLeod."

"Sure, boy, and am I not going to tell you how he got the new name of him?" returned Kirsty. "He wasn't Sir Worm Wymble then. His name was—"

Here she paused a moment, and looked straight at Allister. "His name was Allister—Allister MacLeod."

"Allister!" exclaimed my brother.

"Yes, Allister," said Kirsty. "There's been many an Allister, and not all of them MacLeods, who did what they ought to do, and didn't know what fear was. And you'll be another, I hope," she added, stroking the boy's hair.

Allister's face flushed with pleasure, and it was long before he asked another question.

"Well, as I say," resumed Kirsty, "the girl's father was very angry, and said she should never go and meet Allister again. But the girl did meet him, and told him all about it. And

Allister said nothing much then. But the next day he came striding up to the cottage, at dinnertime, such a big strong gentleman!

" 'Angus MacQueen," says he, 'I understand the kelpie in the pot has been rude to your Nelly. I am going to kill him.'

" 'How will you do that, sir?' said Angus.

" 'Here's a claymore* I could put in a peck,' said Allister, meaning it was such good steel that he could bend it round till the hilt met the point without breaking. 'And here's a shield made out of the hide of the old black bull; and here's a dirk* made of a foot and a half of an old Andrew Ferrara*; and here's a skene dubh* that I'll drive through your door, Mr. Angus. And so we're fitted, I hope.'

" 'Not at all,' said Angus, who as I told you was a wise and knowing man. 'The kelpie's hide is thicker than three bull-hides, and none of your weapons would do more than mark it.'

" 'What am I to do then, Angus, for kill him I will somehow.'

" 'I'll tell you what to do—but it needs a brave man.'

" 'And do you think I'm not brave enough for that, Angus?'

" 'I know one thing you are not brave enough for.'

" 'And what's that?' said Allister, and his face grew red, only he did not want to anger Nelly's father.

" 'You're not brave enough to marry my girl in the face of the clan,' said Angus. 'If my Nelly's good enough to talk to in the glen, she's good enough to lead into the hall before the ladies and gentlemen.'

"Then Allister's face grew redder still, but not with anger, and he held down his head before the old man, but only for a few moments. When he lifted it again, it was pale, not with fear but with resolution, for he had made up his mind.

" 'Mr. Angus MacQueen,' Allister said, 'will you give me your daughter to be my wife?'

" 'If you kill the kelpie, I will,' answered Angus, for he knew that the man who could do that would be worthy of his Nelly."

"But what if the Kelpie ate him?" suggested Allister.

"Then he'd have to go without the girl," said Kirsty, coolly. "But," she resumed, "there's always some way of doing a difficult thing, and Allister the gentleman, had Angus the shepherd, to teach him.

"So Angus took Allister down to the pot. They set great stones together in two rows at a little distance from each other, making a lane between the rows big enough for the kelpie to walk in. If the kelpie heard them, he could not see them, and the two men took care to get into the cottage before it was dark. And they sat up all night, and saw the huge head of the beast looking in now at one window, now at another, all night long. As soon as the sun was up, they set to work again, and finished the two rows of stones all the way from the pot to the top of the little hill on which the cottage stood. Then they tied a cross of rowan twigs on every stone, so that once the beast was in the avenue of stones he could only get out at the end. Next they gathered furze* and brushwood and peat*, and piled it in the end of the avenue next to the cottage. They built up a great heap of stones behind the brushwood, and then Angus went and killed a little pig, and dressed it for cooking.

" 'Now you go down to my brother Hamish the carpenter,' Angus said to Allister, 'and ask him to lend you his longest wimble.' "

"What's a wimble?" asked little Allister.

"A wimble is a long tool, like a great gimlet,* with a cross handle to turn it like a screw. And Allister ran and fetched it, and got back only half an hour before the sun went down. They lit the brushwood, put down the pig to roast by the fire, and laid the wimble in the fire halfway up to the handle. Then they put Nelly into the cottage, and shut the door. Then the two men laid themselves down behind the heap of stones and waited.

"By the time the sun was out of sight, the smell of the roasting pig had drifted down the avenue to the pot. The kelpie thought it smelled so nice that he would go and see where it was. The moment he got out, he was between the stones, but he never thought of that, for it was the straight way to the pig. So up the dark avenue he came on his big, soft, web feet, and the men could not see him until he came into the firelight.

" 'There he is!' said Allister.

" 'Hush!' said Angus, 'he can hear well enough.'

"So the beast came on. Allister drew the wimble gently out of the fire. And while the kelpie was sniffing the pig, Allister thrust that white-hot wimble into the beast's hide and bored away with all his might. The kelpie gave a hideous roar, and turned away to run from the wimble, but he could not get over the row of rowan-crossed stones. Allister hung on to the handle of the wimble, turning it at every chance as the beast floundered on. Before he reached his pot the wimble had reached his heart, and the kelpie fell dead on the edge of the pot! Then they went home, and had the pig for supper. And Angus gave Nelly to Allister, and they were married and they lived happily ever after."

"But didn't Allister's father kill him?"

"No. He thought better of it, and didn't. He was very angry for a while, but he got over it in time. And Allister became a great man, and because of what he had done, he was called Allister MacLeod no more, but Sir Worm Wymble. And when he died," concluded Kirsty, "he was buried under the tomb in your father's church. And if you look close enough, you may find a wimble carved on the stone, though I'm afraid it's worn away by this time."

CHAPTER TEN
The Kelpie

Silence followed Kirsty's tale. Wee Davie was fast asleep. Allister stared into the fire, fancying he saw the whorls of the wimble heating in it. Turkey cut at his stick with a blunt pocketknife, and a silent whistle on his puckered lips. I was sorry the story was over, and was meditating a search for the wimble carved on the knight's tomb. All at once came the sound of a latch lifted in vain, followed by a thundering at the outer door, which Kirsty had prudently locked. Allister, Turkey, and I started to our feet.

"It's the kelpie!" cried Allister.

But Mrs. Mitchell's harsh voice followed. "Kirsty! Open the door directly."

"No, Kirsty!" I objected. "She'll shake wee Davie to bits, and haul Allister through the snow. She's afraid to touch me."

Kirsty carried Davie from the kitchen into the passage between it and the outer door. In that wide passage, which was more like a hall in proportion to the cottage, stood a huge clean barrel. Setting Davie down, she and Turkey lifted first me into it, and then Allister. Finally she took up wee Davie, told him to lie as still as a mouse, and dropped him into our arms. I peeped out through the open bunghole* as the knocking continued.

"Wait a bit, Mrs. Mitchell!" screamed Kirsty. "Wait till I get my potatoes off the fire." As she spoke, she took the great pot in one hand and carried it to the door, to pour away the water.

When she unlocked and opened the door, I saw the moon

shining and the snow falling thick. In the midst of it stood Mrs. Mitchell, who would have rushed in, but Kirsty's advance with the pot made her give way. Then Turkey slipped out from behind Kirsty and around the corner without being seen. There he stood watching, but busy at the same time kneading snowballs.

"And what may you please to want tonight, Mrs. Mitchell?" asked Kirsty, with great civility.

"What should I want but my poor children? They ought to have been in bed an hour ago. Really, Kirsty, you ought to have more sense at your years than to encourage any such goings on."

"At my years!" returned Kirsty, and was about to give a sharp retort, but checked herself. "Aren't they in bed then, Mrs. Mitchell?"

"You know well enough they are not."

"Poor things! I would recommend you to put them to bed at once."

"So I will. Where are they?"

"Find them yourself, Mrs. Mitchell. You had better ask a civil tongue to help you. I'm not going to do it."

They were standing just inside the door. Mrs. Mitchell advanced, and I trembled, for it seemed impossible she should not see me as well as I saw her. She was taller than Kirsty, and by standing on her tiptoes could have looked right down into the barrel. She was approaching it with that intent when a whizz, a dull blow, and a shriek from Mrs. Mitchell came to my ears together. The next moment I saw Mrs. Mitchell holding her head with both hands, and Turkey grinning round the corner of the open door. Turkey was just delivering a second missile when she turned.

That snowball missed her and banged against the barrel. Wee Davie gave a cry of alarm, but there was no danger now, for Mrs. Mitchell was off after Turkey. Kirsty lowered the barrel on its side, and we all crept out. I put wee Davie on my back, Kirsty caught up Allister, and we were off for the manse.

As soon as we were out of the yard, however, we met Turkey, breathless. He had given Mrs. Mitchell the slip, and left her searching the barn for him. He took Allister from Kirsty, and we sped away, for it was all downhill now. When Mrs. Mitchell got back to the farmhouse, Kirsty was busy as if nothing had happened. After a fruitless search, she returned to the manse, where we were all snug in our beds.

From that night Mrs. Mitchell was called by us *the Kelpie.*

CHAPTER ELEVEN
Another Kelpie

In the summer we all slept in a large room in the wide sloping roof. It had a dormer window* just above the eaves. One day there was something doing about the ivy, which covered all the gable and half the front of the house, and the ladder they had been using was left leaning against the back, just under the window. That night I could not sleep, as was frequently the case with me. On such occasions I would wander about the upper part of the house.

The enjoyment it gave me was rooted in the starry loneliness of that night when I woke in the barn. The pleasure arose from a sort of protected danger. On that memorable night, I had been as it were naked to all the silence, alone in the vast universe. But now, when wandering about sleepless, I could gaze from a nest of safety out upon the beautiful fear. From window to window I would go, now staring into the blank darkness alive with rain or hail, now gazing into the deeps of the blue vault gold-bespangled with worlds, now seeing into the mysteries of moonlit clouds.

This night was hot, and my little brothers were sleeping loud—as wee Davie called snoring. I got up, and went to the window. It was such a night! The moon was full, but rather low. All the top of the sky was covered with clouds, and through them the stars shot sharp little rays like sparkling diamonds. This night was not awful, as that other had been. The clouds were like a veil that hid the terrible light in the Holy of Holies—a curtain of God's love, to dim with the loveliness that grandeur of their own being, and make His children able to bear it.

47

I opened the window, crept through, and held on by the ledge. I let myself down over the slates, feeling with my feet for the top of the ladder. Down I went, and oh, how tender to my bare feet was the cool grass on which I alighted!

I went outside the high holly hedge, and the house was hidden. A grassy field was before me, and just beyond the field rose the farm buildings. Why shouldn't I run across and wake Turkey? Turkey slept in a little wooden chamber partitioned off from a loft in the barn, to which he had to climb a ladder. The only fearful part was crossing the barn floor, but I was man enough for that. I reached and crossed the yard in safety, and crossed the barn floor as fast as the darkness would allow me. With outstretched groping hands I found the ladder, ascended, and stood by Turkey's bed.

"Turkey! Turkey! Wake up!" I cried. "It's such a beautiful night! It's a shame to lie sleeping that way."

Turkey was wide awake and out of bed with all his wits by him in a moment.

"Sh! Sh!" he said. "You'll wake Oscar."

Oscar, a collie, slept in a kennel in the corn yard. He was not much of a watchdog, for there was no great occasion for watching. He knew it, and slept like a human child, but he was the most knowing of dogs.

Turkey followed me out into the corn yard. Instead of finding contentment in the sky and moon, he said, "It's not a bad sort of night. What shall we do with it?"

"Oh, nothing," I answered, "only look about us a bit."

"You didn't hear robbers, did you?" he asked.

"Oh dear, no! I couldn't sleep, and got down the ladder, and came to wake you—that's all."

"Let's have a walk, then," he said.

I consented—for now that I had Turkey, there was scarcely more terror in the night than in the day.

As we left the barn, Turkey caught up his little whip. He was never to be seen without either that or his club, as we called the stick he carried when he was herding the cattle. Finding him thus armed, I begged him to give me his club.

He fetched it, and thus equipped, we set out for nowhere in the middle of the night. My fancy was full of fragmentary notions of adventure.

When we arrived at the foot of a wooded hill, well known to all the children of the neighborhood for its bilberries,* he turned into the hollow of a broken track, which lost itself in a field as yet only half-redeemed from the moorland. All at once he stopped, and said, pointing a few yards in front of him, "Look, Ranald!"

He was pointing to the dull gleam of dark, horrible water. It lay in a hollow left by the digging out of peats, drained there from the surrounding bog. My heart sank with fear, and I felt my flesh creep. The almost black glimmer of its surface was bad enough, but who could tell what lay in its unknown depth? Even as we gazed, a huge dark figure rose up on the opposite side of the pool. Despite his unbelief, Kirsty's story must have been working in Turkey's brain that night. He cried out, "The kelpie! The kelpie!" and turned and ran.

I followed as fast as my feet could bear me. We had not gone many yards before a great roar filled the silent air. Turkey slackened his pace, and burst into a fit of laughter. "It's nothing but Bogbonny's bull, Ranald!" he cried. "But he's rather ill-natured, and we had better make for the hill."

Another roar was a fresh spur to our speed. We could not have been in better trim for running, but it was all uphill and the ground was boggy.

"He's caught sight of our shirts," said Turkey, panting as he ran, "and he wants to see what they are. But we'll be over the fence before he catches up with us. I wouldn't mind for myself—I could dodge him well enough—but he might go after you, Ranald."

Another bellow sounded nearer, and we could hear the dull stroke of his hoofs on the soft ground as he galloped after us. But the fence of dry stones was close at hand.

"Over with you, Ranald!" cried Turkey, as if with his last breath. He turned at bay, for the brute was close behind him.

But I was so tired, I could not climb the wall. When I saw Turkey turn and face the bull, I turned too. Turkey lifted his arm, and a short sharp hiss and a roar followed. The bull tossed his head in pain, left Turkey, and came toward me. But Turkey was too quick for him. A second stinging cut from the brass wire drew a second roar from the bull's throat. Then my club descended on one of his horns with a bang which jarred my arm to the elbow and sent the weapon flying over the fence.

The animal turned tail for a moment—long enough for us to jump to the other side of the wall, where we crouched so that he could not see us. Turkey kept looking up at the edge of the wall, and over came the nose of the bull, within a yard of his head. The little whip hissed, and the bull bellowed and fell away. The animal had had enough of us, and we heard no more of him.

We rested for a while, and would have clambered to the top of the hill, but we gave up after getting tangled in a furze bush. In our condition, it was too dark. I began to grow sleepy, and wanted to exchange the hillside for my bed. Turkey made no objection, so we trudged home again—but with many starts and quick glances to make sure that the bull was not after us.

Turkey never left me till he saw me safely up the ladder. Even after I was in bed, I spied his face peeping in at the window. By this time the east had begun to begin to glow (as the painfully exact Allister would have said), but I was fairly tired now, and fell asleep at once.

CHAPTER TWELVE

Wandering Willie

At that time there were many beggars going about the country. Among these were some half-witted persons who, though not to be relied upon, were seldom mischievous. We were not much afraid of them, for the home neighborhood is a charmed spot around which has been drawn a magic circle of safety, and we seldom roamed far beyond it.

But there was one beggar of whom we stood in some degree of awe. He was commonly called Foolish Willie or Wandering Willie. His approach to the manse was always announced by wailing bagpipes, a set of which it was said he had inherited from his father, who had been the piper to some Highland nobleman.

Willie never went anywhere without his pipes, and was more attached to them than to any living creature. He played them well too, and was a great favorite with children especially, despite the mixture of fear which his presence brought to them.

We were always delighted when the far-off sound of Willie's pipes reached us. Little Davie would dance and shout with glee, and even the Kelpie would treat Willie with special kindness. Turkey, who always tried to account for things, declared that Willie must be Mrs. Mitchell's brother, only she was ashamed and wouldn't claim him. She always made sure we saw her filling his canvas bag with any broken scraps she could gather. And she would give him as much milk to drink as he pleased, and would speak kind, almost coaxing, words to him.

Willie's clothing was a mixture of ill-supplied necessity

and superfluous whim. His pleasure was to pin on his person whatever bright colored cotton handkerchiefs he could get hold of. With one of these across his chest and one on his back, he always looked like an ancient herald come with a message from knight or nobleman. He attached bits of old ribbon, list,* and colored rag to his pipes wherever there was room. He looked all flags and pennons*—a moving grove of raggery, out of which came the screaming chant and drone of his instrument. When he danced, he was like a whirlwind that had caught up the contents of an old clothes-shop.

Our first slight fear always gradually wore off, and before the visit was over, wee Davie would be playing with the dangles of his pipes, and laying his ear to the bag. And Willie was particularly fond of Davie, and tried to make himself agreeable to him. The awe, however, was constantly renewed in his absence, partly by the Kelpie's threats to give us to Foolish Willie to take away with him. That threat fell powerless upon me, but still told upon Allister and Davie.

One day in early summer I came home to find that wee Davie had disappeared, and they were looking for him everywhere. Already the farmhouses had been thoroughly searched. The most frightful ideas of Davie's fate arose in my mind, and I sat down upon the grass and cried. In a few minutes, my father rode up on his little black mare.

Mrs. Mitchell hurried to meet him, wringing her hands, and crying, "Oh, sir! Oh, sir! Davie's away with Foolish Willie!"

This was the first I had heard of Willie in connection with Davie. My father turned pale, but asked quietly, "Which way did he go?"

Nobody knew.

"How long ago?"

"About an hour and a half, I think," said Mrs. Mitchell.

To me, the news was some relief. Now I could at least do something. I left the group, and hurried away to find Turkey. Except for my father, I trusted Turkey more than anyone.

The cattle were feeding that afternoon at some distance from home, and I found that Turkey had heard nothing of the mishap. When he understood the dreadful news, he shouldered his club, and said, "The cows must look after themselves, Ranald!"

With the words he set off at a good swinging trot in the direction of a little rocky knoll in a hollow about half a mile away, which he knew to be a favorite haunt of Wandering Willie, as often as he came into the neighborhood. On this knoll grew some stunted trees, gnarled and old, with very mossy stems. There was moss on the stones too, and at the foot of the knoll there were tall foxgloves, which had imparted a certain fear to the spot in my fancy. For there they call them *Dead Man's Bells,* and I thought there was a murdered man buried there. I should not have liked to be there alone even in the broad daylight, but with Turkey I would have gone at any hour. We floundered through some marshy ground between us and the knoll. Then Turkey, who was some distance ahead of me, dropped into a walk, and began to study the knoll with some caution. I soon caught up with him.

"Willie's there, Ranald!" he said. "But I don't know about Davie."

"How do you know?"

"I heard his bagpipes grunt. Perhaps Davie sat down upon them."

"Oh, run, Turkey!" I said, eagerly.

"No hurry," he returned. "If Willie has Davie, he won't hurt him, but it may not be easy to get him away. We must creep up and see what can be done."

Half dead as some of the trees were, there was foliage enough upon them to hide Willie; Turkey hoped it would hide us as well. He went down on his hands and knees, and thus crept toward the knoll. I followed his example, and when we reached the steep side, we lay still and listened. A weary whimper as of a child worn out with hopeless crying reached our ears.

"He's there!" I cried in a whisper.

"Sh!" said Turkey. "I hear him. It's all right. We'll soon have a hold of him." He immediately began to climb the side of the knoll. "Stay where you are, Ranald," he said. "I can go up quieter than you."

I obeyed. Cautious as a deerstalker, Turkey ascended on his hands and knees. But when he was near the top he lay perfectly quiet, till I could bear it no longer, and crept up after him. When I came behind him, he looked around angrily. I dared not climb to a level with him, but lay trembling with expectation.

The next moment I heard him call in a low whisper, "Davie! Wee Davie!"

But there was no reply. Turkey called a little louder, trying to reach Davie's ears and not Willie's. At length a small trembling voice cried, "Turkey!" in mingled hope and pain.

Turkey sprang to his feet and vanished. I followed, but before I reached the top, there came a despairing cry from Davie, and a shout and a gabble from Willie. Then followed a louder shout and a louder gabble, mixed with a scream from the bagpipes, and an exulting laugh from Turkey.

I reached the top and saw Davie alone in the thicket, Turkey scudding down the opposite slope with the bagpipes under his arm, and Wandering Willie pursuing him in a foaming fury. I caught Davie in my arms from where he lay sobbing and crying, "Yanal! Yanal!"

Turkey led Willie toward the deepest of the boggy ground, in which both were very soon floundering—but Turkey, being the lighter, had the advantage. I made for home with Davie on my back, and slid down the farther side to skirt the bog. I had not gone far, however, before a howl from Willie made me aware that he had caught sight of us. Looking around, I saw him turn from Turkey and come after us. But Willie hesitated, then stopped, and began looking this way and that from the one to the other of his treasures, both in evil hands.

He made up his mind far too soon, for he chose to follow Davie. I ran my best in the very strength of despair for some distance, but, seeing that I had no chance, I set Davie down, told him to keep behind me, and prepared for battle. Willie came on in fury, his rags fluttering like ten scarecrows, and he waving his arms in the air with wild gestures and grimaces and cries and curses. He was more terrible than the bull, and Turkey was behind him.

I was just preparing to run my head into the pit of Willie's stomach, when I saw Turkey running toward us at full speed, blowing into the bagpipes as he ran. How he found breath for both I cannot understand. At length, he put the bag under his arm, and issued such a combination of screeching and grunting and howling, that Willie turned at the cries of his companion.

Then came Turkey's masterpiece. He dashed the bagpipes on the ground, and began kicking them like a football, and the pipes cried out at every kick. This was more than Willie could bear; he turned from us and once again pursued his pipes. When Willie had nearly overtaken him, Turkey gave the pipes a last masterly kick, caught them up, and again sought the bog. I hoisted Davie on my back and hurried toward the manse.

I never looked behind me till I reached the little green before the house. There I set Davie down, and threw myself on the grass. I remember nothing more till I came to myself in bed.

Turkey told me later that when he reached the bog, and had lured Wandering Willie well into the middle of it, he threw the bagpipes as far beyond him as he could, and then made his way out. Willie followed the pipes, took them, and held them up between him and the sky as if appealing to heaven against the cruelty. Then he sat down in the middle of the bog upon a solitary hump, and cried like a child. Turkey stood and watched him, at first with feelings of triumph, which cooled down into compassion. He grew heartily sorry for the poor fellow, although there was no room for repentance. After Willie had cried for a while, he took the instrument as if it had been the mangled corpse of his son, and proceeded to examine it. Turkey declared that none of the pipes were broken, but when Willie put the mouthpiece to his lips, and began to blow into the bag, alas! It would hold no wind. Turkey left him crying in the middle of the bog.

It was long before Willie appeared in that part of the country again. About six months later, some neighbors who had been to a fair twenty miles off, told my father that they had seen Willie looking much as usual, and playing his pipes with more energy than ever. This was a great relief to my father, who could not bear the idea of the poor fellow's loneliness without his pipes, and had wanted very much to get them repaired for him. But ever after that my father showed a great regard for Turkey. I heard him say once that, if he had the chance, Turkey would make a great general. That he should be judged so capable was not surprising to me.

When I came to myself, I was in my father's bed with a sharp pain in my side, and I could draw but a very short breath for it. There was no one in the room, but soon my father came in, and then I felt that all was as it should be. Seeing me awake, he approached with an anxious face.

"Is Davie all right, Father?" I asked.

"He is quite well, Ranald, my boy. How do you feel yourself now?"

"I've been asleep, Father?"

"Yes—we found you on the grass, with Davie pulling at you to wake you, crying, 'Yanal won't peak to me. Yanal!' I am afraid you had a terrible run with him. Turkey, as you call him, told me all about it. He's a fine lad!"

"Indeed he is, Father!" I cried with a gasp.

"What is the matter, my boy?" he asked.

"Lift me up a little, please," I said. "I have *such* a pain in my side!"

"Ah!" he said. "We must send for the old doctor."

The old doctor was a sort of demigod in the place. Everyone believed and trusted in him, and nobody could die in peace without him any more than without my father. I was delighted at the thought of being his patient.

That night I was delirious, and haunted by bagpipes. Wandering Willie was nowhere, but the atmosphere was full of bagpipes. It was an unremitting storm of bagpipes—silent, but assailing me from all quarters—now small as motes in the sun, and hailing upon me; then large as featherbeds, and ready to bang us about; finally huge as a mountain, and threatening to smother us beneath their ponderous bulk. And all the time I was toiling with Davie on my back.

The next day I was very weak, and it was many days before I was able to get out of bed. My father soon found that it would not do to let Mrs. Mitchell tend to me, for I was always worse after she had been in the room. So another woman took Kirsty's duties, and Kirsty nursed me, after which illness almost became a luxury. With Kirsty near, nothing could go wrong.

Once, when Kirsty was absent, Mrs. Mitchell brought me some gruel. I pronounced it not nice; Kirsty returned, and said it was not fit for anyone. She carried it away, and Mrs. Mitchell followed her with her nose horizontal. Kirsty brought back some delicious gruel, well boiled, and supplemented with cream. It was done as well as it could be done, and everything well done is something for the progress of the world.

On a delightful glowing summer afternoon I was carried out to the field where Turkey was herding the cattle. I could not yet walk. I was so light from the wasting illness, that Kirsty herself, little woman as she was, was able to carry me. I saw everything double that day, and found it at first very amusing. Kirsty set me down on a plaid* in the grass, and the next moment, Turkey, looking awfully big and healthy, stood by my side.

"Eh, Ranald!" said Turkey. "It's not yourself?"

"It's me, Turkey," I said, nearly crying with joy.

"Never mind, Ranald," he returned, as if consoling me in some disappointment. "We'll have rare fun yet."

"I'm frightened at the cows, Turkey. Don't let them come near me."

"No, that I won't," answered Turkey, brandishing his club to give me confidence. "I'll give it to them if they look at you from between their ugly horns."

"Turkey," I said, for I had often pondered the matter, "how did Hawkie behave while you were away with me that day?"

"She ate about half a rick of green corn," answered Turkey, coolly. "But she had the worst of it. They had to make a hole in her side, or she would have died. There she is off to the turnips!"

He was after her with a shout and a flourish. Hawkie heard and obeyed, turning round on her hind legs with a sudden start, for she knew from his voice that he was in a dangerously energetic mood.

"You'll be all right again soon," he said, coming quietly back to me.

"I'm nearly well now, only I can't walk yet."

"Will you climb on my back?" he said.

So I followed the cows on Turkey's back, riding him about wherever I chose; my horse was obedient as only a dog, or a horse, or a servant from love can be. From that day I recovered very rapidly.

CHAPTER THIRTEEN
Elsie Duff

Now I had gone to school for some months before I was taken ill—a very different school from Dame Shand's tyrannical little kingdom. Here were boys and girls of all ages, ruled over by Mr. Wilson, an energetic and enthusiastic young master with a touch of genius.

He spoke to me kindly, and he roused in me a love for English literature, especially poetry. After a day of work, it is still a great comfort to return to my books, and live in the company of those who were greater than myself, and had a higher work in life than mine. The master used to say that a man was fit company for any man whom he could understand, and therefore I hope that someday I may look upon the faces of Milton* and Bacon* and Shakespeare—men whose writings have given me so much strength and hope.

When I returned to school after my adventure, how all the boys and girls stared at me! I entered timidly, yet with a sense of importance derived from the distinction of having been so ill. The master came up to me and took me by the hand, saying he was glad to see me at school again. I worked hard, but before the morning was over, I fell asleep with my head on the desk. I was told afterward that the master had interfered when one of my classmates was trying to wake me, and told him to let me sleep.

When one o'clock came, I was roused by the noise of dismissal for the two hours for dinner. I staggered out, still sleepy, and whom should I find watching for me by the door but Turkey!

"Turkey!" I exclaimed. "You here?"

"Yes, Ranald," he said. "I've put the cows up for an hour or two, for it was very hot, and Kirsty said I might come to carry you home."

He stooped and took me on his strong back. Then he turned his head and said, "Ranald, I should like to go and see my mother. Will you come? There's plenty of time."

"Yes, please, Turkey," I answered. "I've never seen your mother."

He set off at a slow easy trot, and bore me through street and lane until we arrived at a two-story house, where his mother lived in the garret.* She was a widow, and had only Turkey. What a curious place her little garret was! The roof sloped down on one side to the very floor, and there was a little window in it, from which I could see away to the manse—a mile off—and far beyond it. Her bed stood in one corner, and in another was a chest.

Turkey's mother was sitting near the little window spinning. She was a thin, sad-looking woman, with loving eyes and slow speech.

"Johnnie!" she exclaimed. "What brings you here? And who's this you've brought with you?"

Instead of stopping her work as she spoke, she made her wheel go faster than before, and I admired her deft fingering of the wool. The thread flowed out in a continuous line toward the revolving spool.

"It's Ranald Bannerman," said Turkey quietly. "I'm his horse. I'm taking him home from school, for this is the first day he's been there since he was ill."

She relaxed her labor, and the spinning hooks, which had been revolving invisible in a mist of motion, began to reveal their shape, and at last stood quite still. She rose, and said, "Come, Master Ranald, and sit down. You'll be tired of riding such a rough horse as that."

"No, indeed," I said. "Turkey's not rough—he's the best horse in all the world."

"He always calls me Turkey, Mother, because of my nose," said Turkey, laughing.

"And what brings you here?" asked his mother. "This is not the road to the manse."

"I wanted to see if you were better, Mother."

"But what becomes of the cows?"

"Oh! They're all safe enough. They know I'm here."

"Well, sit down and rest you both," she said, resuming her place at the wheel. "I'm glad to see you, Johnnie, so be your work is not neglected. I must go on with mine."

Turkey deposited me on the bed, and sat down beside me.

"And how's your papa, the good man?" she asked me.

I told her he was quite well.

"All the better that you're restored from the grave, I don't doubt," she said.

I had not known that I had been in any danger.

"It's been a sore time for him and you too," she added. "You must be a good son to him, Ranald, for he was a great way worried about you, they tell me."

Turkey said nothing, and I was too much surprised to know what to say, for my father had always looked cheerful, and I had no idea that he was uneasy about me.

After a little more talk, Turkey rose, and said we must be going.

"Well, Ranald," said his mother, "you must come and see me any time when you're tired at the school, and you can lie down and rest yourself a bit. Be a good lad, Johnnie, and mind your work."

"Yes, Mother, I'll try," answered Turkey cheerfully, as he hoisted me once more upon his back. "Good day, Mother," he added, and we left the room.

I rode home upon Turkey's back, and with my father's permission, instead of returning to school that day, spent the afternoon in the fields with Turkey.

In the middle of the field where the cattle were that day, there was a large circular mound. It must have been a barrow, with dead men's bones in the heart of it, but no such suspicion had then crossed my mind. On the steep grassy side farthest from the manse, and without one human dwelling in sight, Turkey and I lay that afternoon. My bliss was enhanced by the thought of the close, hot, dusty school-room, where my class-fellows were talking, laughing and wrangling, or perhaps trying to work. A fitful little breeze would wave a few heads of horse-daisies, waft a few strains of odor from the blossoms of the white clover, and then die away fatigued. Turkey took out his Jew's harp* and produced soothing if not eloquent strains.

At our feet ran a babbling brook which divided our farm from the next. This brook sung in a veiled voice, muffled in the hollows of overhanging banks, with a low, musical gurgle in some of the stony eddies. The brook was deep for its size, and had a good deal to say in a solemn tone for such a small stream.

We lay on the side of the mound, and Turkey's harp mingled its sounds with those of the brook. After a while he laid it aside, and we were both silent.

Finally Turkey spoke. "You've seen my mother, Ranald. She's all I've got to look after."

"I haven't got any mother to look after, Turkey."

"No, but you have a father to look after you. I must do it, you know. My father wasn't very good to my mother. He used to get drunk sometimes, and then he was very rough with her. I must make it up to her as well as I can. She's not well off, Ranald. She works very hard at her spinning, and no one spins better than my mother. But it's very poor pay, you know, and she'll be getting old by and by."

"Not tomorrow, Turkey."

"No, not tomorrow, nor the day after," said Turkey, looking up with some surprise to see what I meant by the remark.

He then discovered that my eyes had led my thoughts astray, and that what he had been saying about his mother had gone no farther than my ears. On the grass on the opposite side of the stream sat a young girl about my own age, in the midst of a crowded colony of daisies and white clover. She was knitting so that her needles went as fast as

Kirsty's, and were nearly invisible. A little way from her was a fine cow feeding, with a long iron chain dragging after her.

"Oh! There's Elsie Duff, with her grannie's cow!" said Turkey, himself forgetting his mother in the sight. "I didn't know she was coming here today."

"How is it," I asked, "that she is feeding her on old James Joss' land?"

"Oh! They're very good to Elsie, though nobody cares much about her grandmother. The cow belongs to the old woman, yet for Elsie's sake, this farmer or that one generally gives her a day's feed. She's as plump as needful, and has a good udderful of milk besides."

"I'll run down and tell her she may bring the cow into this field tomorrow," I said, rising.

"I would if it were mine," said Turkey, in a marked tone, which I understood.

"Oh! I see, Turkey. You mean I ought to ask my father."

"Yes, to be sure," answered Turkey.

"Then I will ask him tonight," I returned.

"She's a good girl, Elsie," was all Turkey's reply.

Yet I failed to ask my father, and Granny Gregson's cow had no bite from either the glebe or the farm.

I soon grew quite strong again, and had no reason or desire for freedom from schoolwork. My father had begun to take me in hand as well as my brother Tom, and what with arithmetic and Latin and geography and history, I had quite as much to do as was good for me.

CHAPTER FOURTEEN

A New Companion

During this summer, I met Peter Mason, a clever boy with merry eyes. He seldom knew his lesson well, but, when kept in for not knowing it, had always learned it before any of the rest were more than half through. Among those of his own standing he was the acknowledged leader in the playground, and was besides often invited to share in the amusements of the older boys. Beyond school hours, Peter spent his time in all manner of pranks. In the hot summer weather he would bathe twenty times a day, and was much at home in the water. And that was how I came to be more with him than was good for me.

There was a small river not far from my father's house, which at a certain point was dammed back by a stone weir* to turn part of it aside into a millrace. The mill stood a little way down, under a steep bank. It was almost surrounded with willows by the water's edge, and birches and larches up the bank. Above the dam was a fine spot for bathing, for you could get any depth you liked—from two feet to six. Here it was that most of the boys of the village bathed, and I with them.

God must love His little children to have invented for them such delights! If He did not love the children and delight in their pleasure, He would not have invented the two and brought them together.

One day, a good many of us were at the water. I bathed off my father's ground, while the other boys were all on a piece of the opposite bank. But when they were all undressed, and some already in the water, there suddenly appeared a man who had lately rented that property. He was accompanied by a villainous-looking mongrel dog, and ordered everyone off his premises. Invaded with terror, all, except one big boy, plunged into the river, and swam away from the hostile shore. Once in the embrace of the stream, some of the boys thoughtlessly turned and mocked the enemy.

Indignant at the tyrant, I assured the boys of a welcome on the opposite bank. But their clothes were upon the riverbank they had left! The spirit of a host was upon me, for now I regarded them all as my guests. "You come ashore when you like," I said. "I will see what can be done about your clothes."

Just below the dam lay a little clumsy boat built by the miller's sons. On the opposite shore stood the big boy braving the low-bred cur which barked and growled at him with its ugly head stretched out like a serpent's. The dog's owner, who was probably not so unkind as we thought him, stood enjoying the fun of it all. Reckoning upon the big boy's help, I scrambled out of the water, and sped for the boat. I jumped in and seized the oars, intending to row across, and get the big boy to throw all the clothes in the boat. But I had never handled an oar in my life, and I soon fell from the boat.

Now, the water below the dam was deeper here than in almost any other part, and there were horrors afloat concerning its depth. I was but a poor swimmer, for swimming is a natural gift, and is not equally distributed to all. I was struggling and floundering, half-blind, and quite deaf, with the water constantly getting up and stopping whatever I wanted to do, when something laid hold of my leg, dragged me under the water, and landed me safely on the bank again.

I heard a plunge, and saw a boy swimming after the boat. I saw him overtake it, scramble into it in midstream, and handle the oars as to the manner born. When he had brought it back to the spot where I stood, I realized that Peter Mason was my deliverer. Quite recovered by this time from my slight attack of drowning, I got again into the boat, left the oars to Peter, and was rowed across. There was no further difficulty. The man, alarmed at the danger I had run, recalled his dog. Then we bundled the clothes into the boat, and Peter rowed them across.

For the whole of that summer and part of the following winter, Peter was my hero, to the forgetting even of my friend Turkey. I took every opportunity to join Peter in his games—partly from gratitude, partly from admiration. It was some time before he led me into any real mischief, but it came at last.

CHAPTER FIFTEEN
Down Hill

It came in the following winter.

My father had now begun to teach me as well as Tom, but I confess I did not then value the privilege. I had grown much too fond of Peter Mason, and all the time I could command I spent with him. Always full of questionable frolic, the joys of summer kept him within bounds. But when the ice and snow came, when the wind was full of frost and the ground was hard as a stone, when the evenings were dark, and the sun at noon shone low down and far away in the south, then the demon of mischief awoke in Peter Mason—and, this winter, I am ashamed to say, drew me also into the net.

It was a Friday in January, and the sun set about half past three. When school was over at three, Peter whispered to me, a merry twinkle in his eyes, "Come across after dark, Ranald, and we'll have some fun."

We arranged when and where to meet. After dinner, I was impatient to join Peter, and from very idleness began to tease wee Davie. Poor Davie began to cry, and I went on teasing him, until he burst into a howl of wrath and misery, whereupon the Kelpie burst into the room, and boxed my ears soundly. In spite of my rage and resistance, she pushed me out of the room and locked the door. I would have complained to my father, but I was perfectly aware that I deserved chastisement for my behavior. I was still boiling with anger when I set off for the village.

I was in a bad state of mind, and thus prepared for wickedness. A boy never disgraces himself all at once. He does not tumble from the top to the bottom of the cellar stair. He goes down the steps himself till he comes to the broken one, and then he goes to the bottom with a rush.

There were very few people about in the village. The night was very cold, for there was a black frost. A thaw the day before had carried away most of the snow, but in the corners lay dirty heaps which had been swept up there. I was waiting near one of these for Peter, when a girl came out from a shop and walked quickly down the street. I yielded to the temptation arising in a mind which had grown dark; I scraped out a handful of dirty snow, kneaded it into a snowball, and sent it flying after the girl. It struck her on the back of the head, and she gave a cry and ran away with her hand to her forehead.

Brute that I was, I actually laughed. I think I must have been nearer the devil then than I have been since. I knew quite well that I was doing wrong, and refused to think about it, though I felt bad inside. The vile dregs of my wrath with the Kelpie were fermenting in my heart, but I was more displeased with myself than with anybody else. But I did not admit it, and would not take the trouble to repent and do the right thing. If I had even said to wee Davie that I was sorry, I do not think I should have done the other wicked things that followed.

In a little while Peter joined me. He laughed when I told him how the girl had run like a frightened hare, but that was poor fun in his eyes.

"Look here, Ranald," he said, holding out a cabbage stalk. "I've scooped out the inside and filled it with tow.* We'll set fire to one end, and blow the smoke through the keyhole."

"Whose keyhole, Peter?"

"An old witch's that I know of. She'll be in such a rage! It'll be fun to hear her cursing and swearing. Come along— here's a rope to tie her door with."

I followed him, not without inward misgivings, which I kept down as well as I could. I argued with myself, *I am not doing it—I am only going with Peter, and won't touch the thing myself.* A few minutes later I was helping Peter tie the rope to the latch handle, saying now to myself, *This won't do her any harm. This isn't smoke. And after all, smoke won't hurt the nasty old thing. It'll only make her angry. It may do her cough good. I dare say she has a cough.*

I knew all I was saying was false, and yet I acted on it. Was not that as wicked as wickedness could be? One moment more, and Peter was blowing through the hollow cabbage stalk in at the keyhole with all his might. Catching a breath of the stifling smoke himself, however, he began to cough violently, and passed the wicked instrument to me. I put my mouth to it, and blew with all my might. I believe now that there was some far more objectionable stuff mingled with the tow. In a few moments, the old woman began to cough. Peter, who was peeping in at the window, whispered, "She's rising. Now we'll catch it, Ranald!"

She shuffled toward the door, coughing as she came, thinking to open it for air. When she failed in opening it, and found besides where the smoke was coming from, she broke into a torrent of fierce and vengeful reproaches. She did not curse and swear as Peter had led me to expect, although her language was far from refined.

I laughed because I would not be unworthy of my companion, who was genuinely amused, but I was shocked at the tempest I had raised. I stopped blowing, aghast at what I had done, but Peter caught the tube from my hand and began to blow again, whispering through the keyhole between the blasts, making provoking remarks on the old woman's personal appearance and supposed ways of living. This threw her into fits of rage and of coughing, both increasing in violence. As the war of words grew, she tugged at the door and screamed, while he answered merrily, and with pretended sympathy for her sufferings. I lost all remaining delicacy in the humor of the wicked game, and laughed loud and heartily.

Then suddenly the scolding and coughing ceased. A strange sound followed, and then silence. Then came a shrill, suppressed scream, and we heard the voice of a girl crying, "Grannie! Grannie! What's the matter with you? Can't you speak to me, Grannie? They've smothered my grannie!"

Sobs and moans were all we heard now. Peter had taken fright at last, and was busy undoing the rope. Suddenly, he flung the door wide and fled, leaving me exposed to the full gaze of the girl. It was Elsie Duff! She was just approaching the door, her eyes streaming with tears, and her sweet face white with agony. I stood unable to move or speak. She turned away without a word, and began again to tend to the old woman, who lay on the ground not two yards from the door. I fled at full speed—not to find Peter, but to leave everything behind me.

When I reached the manse, it stood alone in the starry blue night. Somehow I could not help thinking of the time when I came home after waking up in the barn. That too was a time of misery, but, oh, how different from this! Then I had only been cruelly treated myself; now I had actually committed cruelty. Then I sought my father's bosom as the one refuge; now I dreaded the very sight of my father, for I could not look him in the face. He was my father, but I was not his son. I became more and more miserable as I stood, but the cold at length drove me into the house.

I generally sat with my father in his study, but I dared not go near it now. I crept to the nursery, where I found a bright fire burning, and Allister reading by the blaze, while Davie lay in bed at the other side of the room. I sat down and warmed myself, but the warmth could not reach the lump of ice in my heart. Allister was too occupied with his book to notice me. Then I felt a pair of arms around my neck as Davie tried to climb upon my knees. Instead of being comforted, however, I spoke very crossly, and sent him back to his bed whimpering. I was only miserable; I was not repentant.

How I got through the rest of that evening I hardly know. I tried to read, but could not. I was rather fond of arithmetic, so I got my slate and tried to work a sum, but in a few moments I was sick of it. At family prayers I never lifted my head to look at my father, and when they were over, and I had said good-night to him, I felt that I was sneaking out of the room. But I had some small sense of protection and safety when once in bed beside little Davie, who was sound asleep, and looked as innocent as little Samuel when the voice of God was going to call him. I put my arm around Davie, hugged him close, and began to cry. The crying brought me sleep.

It was a very long time now since I had dreamt my old childish dream, but this night it returned. The old sun looked down upon me very solemnly. There was no smile on his big mouth, no twinkle about the corners of his little eyes. He looked at Mrs. Moon as much as to say, "What *is* to be done? The boy has been going the wrong way. Must we disown him?" The moon turned and stood with her back to her husband, looking very miserable. The star-children did not move from their places, but shone sickly and small. In a little while they faded out; then the moon paled and vanished without ever turning her face to her husband. Finally the sun himself began to change. He drew in all his beams, and shrunk smaller and smaller, until he was no bigger than a candle flame. Then I found that I was staring at a candle on the table, and that Tom was kneeling by the side of the other bed, saying his prayers.

CHAPTER SIXTEEN

The Trouble Grows

When I woke in the morning, I tried to persuade myself that I had done at worst but a boy's trick. And I would have no more to say to Peter Mason, who had betrayed me at the last moment. I went to school as usual. It was the day for the Shorter Catechism. None failed but Peter and me, and we were kept in together.

In half an hour he had learned his task, while I had not mastered the half of mine. Thereupon Peter proceeded to prevent me from learning it. I begged, and appealed to his pity, but he would pull the book away from me, gabble ballads in my ear, and tip up the form I was seated on. At last I began to cry, for Peter was a bigger and stronger boy than I. Then I thought I saw a shadow pass from the window. I was convinced it was Turkey, and my heart began to turn again toward him. Peter grew suddenly weary of the sport, and said, "Ranald, you can stay if you like. I've learned my catechism, and I don't see why I should wait."

As he spoke, he drew a picklock from his pocket, deliberately opened the schoolroom door, slipped out, and locked it behind him. Then he came to one of the windows, and began making faces at me. But vengeance was nearer than he knew. There was Turkey towering over Peter, with his hand on his collar and his whip lifted. Peter laughed in Turkey's face and wriggled free, but Turkey's whip came down upon him. With a howl of pain Peter doubled himself up, and Turkey fell upon him, and, heedless of his yells and cries, pommelled him severely. Peter soon crept past the window, a miserable mass of collapsed impudence, his face bleared with crying, and his knuckles dug into his eyes. And this was the boy I had chosen for my leader! He had been false to me, and the noble Turkey had watched to give him his desserts. My heart was full of gratitude.

Once more Turkey drew near the window. But I was dismayed to hear him say, "If you weren't your father's son, Ranald, and my own old friend, I would serve you the same."

Wrath and pride arose in me. My evil ways having half made a sneak of me, I cried out, "I'll tell my father!"

"I wish you would! Then I should be no tell-tale if he asked me, and I told him all about it. You young blackguard! You're no gentleman! To sneak about the streets and hit girls with snowballs! I scorn you!"

"You must have been watching, then, Turkey, and you had no business to do that," I said, plunging at any defense.

"I was not watching you. But if I had been, it would have been just as right as watching Hawkie. You ill-behaved creature! I met Elsie Duff crying in the street because you had hit her with a dirty snowball. And then to go and smoke her and her poor grannie, till the old woman fell down in a faint or a fit! You deserve a good pommelling yourself, Ranald. I'm ashamed of you!"

He turned to go away.

"Turkey!" I cried. "Isn't the old woman better?"

"I don't know. I'm going to see," he answered.

"Come back and tell me, Turkey!" I shouted, as he disappeared.

"Indeed I won't. I don't choose to keep company with such as you. But if I ever hear of you touching them again, you shall have more of me than you'll like. You may tell your father so when you please."

I had indeed sunk low when my friend Turkey would have nothing more to say to me. The master soon returned, found me crying, and was touched with compassion. He sent me home at once, which was well for me, for I could not have repeated a single question. He thought Peter had crept through one of the panes that opened for ventilation, and did not ask me about him.

The rest of that day was miserable. I could bear no company, and went to bed the moment prayers were over. I slept a troubled sleep, and dreamed that Turkey had told my father, and that my father had turned me out of the house.

CHAPTER SEVENTEEN
Light Out Of Darkness

I woke early on the Sunday morning, and a most dreary morning it was. I could not lie in bed, and so rose and dressed. I passed through the silent house and went out the front door. The dark dead frost held the day in chains of iron. The sky was dull and leaden, and cindery flakes of snow fell thinly. All life looked utterly dreary and hopeless. I went out on the road, and the ice in the ruts crackled under my feet like the bones of dead things. I wandered away from the house, and the keen wind cut me to the bone. I turned into a field, and stumbled along over its uneven frozen surface. The summer was gone and the winter was here, and my heart was old and miserable.

I came to the hill where Turkey and I had lain on that lovely afternoon the year before. The stream below was dumb with frost, and the wind blew wearily but sharply across the bare field. There was no Elsie Duff seated in the summer grass across the singing brook. Her head was aching on her pillow because I had struck her with that vile lump, and instead of the odor of white clover she was breathing the dregs of the hateful smoke with which I had filled the cottage. I sat down, cold as it was, and buried my face in my hands. Then my dream returned—this was how I sat in my dream when my father had turned me out of the house!

I could not sit long in the cold, and grew so wretched in body that I forgot for a while the trouble of my mind. I wandered home again, and the house was just stirring. I crept to the nursery, undressed, and lay down beside little

Davie, who cried out in his sleep when my cold feet touched him. But I did not sleep again, although I lay till all the rest had gone to the parlor. I found them seated around a blazing fire waiting for my father. He came in soon after, and we had our breakfast. I fancied my father's eyes were often turned in my direction, but I could not lift mine to make sure. I had never before known what misery was.

It was so cold that day that only Tom and I went to church. My father preached from the text, "Be sure your sin shall find you out." I thought that he had found out *my* sin, and was preparing to punish me for it. I was filled with terror as well as dismay. But after telling many instances in which punishment had come upon evildoers when they least expected it, and in spite of every precaution to fortify themselves against it, Papa said that a man's sin might find him out long before the punishment of it overtook him. He drew a picture of the misery of the wicked man who fled when none pursued him, and trembled at the rustling of a leaf. Then I was certain that he knew what I had done, or had seen through my face into my conscience.

I waited the whole of that day for the storm to break, expecting every moment to be called to Papa's study. I did not enjoy a mouthful of my food, for I felt his eyes upon me, and they tortured me. I had nowhere to hide, and my very soul was naked! After tea I slunk away to the nursery, and sat staring into the fire. At length Mrs. Mitchell brought Davie in and put him to bed. Then I heard my father coming down the stairs with Allister.

My father came in with the big Bible under his arm, as was his custom on Sunday nights. He drew a chair to the table, and with Allister by his side and me seated opposite him, read through without a word of remark the Parable of the Prodigal Son. When he came to the father's delight at having him back, the robe, and the shoes, and the ring, I could not repress my tears. *If only I could go back,* I thought, *and set it all right!* It was a foolish thought, instantly followed by a long impulse to tell my father all about it. Why had I not thought of it before? I had been waiting all this time for my sin to find me out—why should I not frustrate my sin, and find my father first?

As soon as he had finished reading, and before he had opened his mouth to make any remark, I crept around the table to his side, and whispered in his ear, "Papa, I want to speak to you."

"Very well, Ranald," he said, more solemnly than usual. "Come up to the study."

He rose, and a whimper of disappointment came from Davie's bed. My father went and kissed him, and said he would soon be back, and Davie nestled down satisfied.

When we reached the study, Papa closed the door, sat down by the fire, and drew me toward him. I burst out crying. He encouraged me most kindly, and said, "Have you been doing anything wrong, my boy?"

"Yes, Papa, very wrong," I sobbed. "I'm disgusted with myself."

"I am glad to hear it, my dear," he returned. "There is some hope for you, then."

"Oh, I don't know that," I rejoined. "Even Turkey despises me."

"That's very serious," said my father. "He's a fine fellow, and I should not like him to despise me. But tell me about it."

After some questioning, my father understood the whole matter. He thought for a while, then rose, saying, "It's a serious affair, my dear boy. But now that you have told me, I shall be able to help you."

"But you knew about it before, didn't you, Papa?"

"Not a word of it, Ranald. You fancied so because your sin had found you out. I must go and see how the poor woman is. I don't want to reproach you at all, now that you are sorry, but I want you to know that you have been helping to make that poor old woman wicked. She is naturally of a sour disposition, and you have made it sourer still, and no doubt made her hate everybody more than she already did. You have been working against God in this parish."

I burst into fresh tears. "What am I to do?" I cried.

"You must beg Mrs. Gregson's pardon, and tell her that you are both sorry and ashamed."

"Yes, yes, Papa. Do let me go with you."

"It's too late to find her up, I'm afraid. But we can go and see. We've done a wrong, a very grievous wrong, my boy. I cannot rest till I at least know the end of it."

He hastened on his long coat and muffler, and saw that I too was properly wrapped up. He opened the door and stepped out. But remembering the promise he had made to Davie, he turned and went down to the nursery again, while I waited on the doorstep. It would have been quite dark but for the stars, and there was no snow to give back any of their shine. The earth swallowed all their rays, and was no brighter for it. But oh, what a change to me from the frightened morning! When my father returned, I put my hand fearlessly in his, and away we walked together.

"Papa," I said, "why did you say *we* have done a wrong? *You* did not do it."

"My dear boy, persons who are so near each other as we are, must not only bear the consequences together of any wrong done by one of them, but must, in a sense, bear each other's iniquities. If I sin, you must suffer; if you sin, I must suffer. And it is up to both of us to do what we can to get rid of the wrong done, and thus we have to bear each other's sin. I am accountable to make amends as far as I can—and also to do what I can to get you to be sorry and make amends as far as you can."

"But, Papa, isn't that hard?"

"Do you think I should like to leave you to get out of your sin as best you could, or to sink deeper and deeper into it? Don't you think I should want to be troubled about it? Or if I were to do anything wrong, would you think it very hard that you had to help me to be good, and set things right? Even if people looked down upon you because of me, would you say it was hard? Would you not rather say, 'I'm glad to bear anything for my father—I'll share it with him'?"

"Yes, indeed, Papa. I would rather share with you than not, whatever it was."

"Then you see, my boy, how kind God is in tying us up in one bundle that way. It is a grand and beautiful thing that the fathers should suffer for the children, and the children for the fathers. But I fear we shall not be able to make our apology tonight. When we've got over this, Ranald, we must be a good deal more careful what company we keep."

"O Papa," I said, "if Turkey would only forgive me!"

"There's no fear. Turkey is sure to forgive you when you've done what you can to make amends."

"If he would, Papa, I should not wish for any other company than his."

"A boy wants various kinds of companions, Ranald, but I fear you have been neglecting Turkey. You owe him much."

"Indeed I do, Papa," I answered, "and I have been neglecting him. If I had kept with Turkey, I should never have gotten into such a dreadful scrape as this."

"That is too light a word to use for it, my boy. Don't call a wickedness a scrape, for a wickedness it certainly was, though I believe you had no idea at the time *how* wicked it was."

"I won't again, Papa. But I am so relieved already."

"Perhaps poor old Mrs. Gregson is not relieved, though. You ought not to forget her."

Thus talking, we hurried on to the cottage. A dim light was visible through the window. My father knocked, and Elsie Duff opened the door.

CHAPTER EIGHTEEN

Forgiveness

When we entered, there sat the old woman on the farther side of the hearth, rocking herself to and fro. I hardly dared look up. Elsie's face was composed and sweet, and she gave me a shy tremulous smile, which went to my heart and humbled me dreadfully. My father took the stool on which Elsie had been sitting. When he had lowered himself upon it, his face was nearly on a level with that of the old woman, who took no notice of him, but kept rocking and moaning. He laid his hand on hers, which, old and withered and not very clean, lay on her knee.

"How do you find yourself tonight, Mrs. Gregson?" he asked.

"I'm an ill-used woman," she replied with a groan, behaving as if it was my father who had maltreated her, and whose duty it was to apologize.

"I am aware of what you mean, Mrs. Gregson. That is what brought me to inquire after you. I hope you are not seriously the worse for it."

"I'm an ill-used woman," she repeated. "Every man's hand's against me."

"Well, I hardly think that," said my father in a cheerful tone. "*My* hand's not against you."

"If you bring up your sons, Mr. Bannerman, to mock at the poor, and find their amusement in driving the aged and infirm to death's door, you can't say your hand's not against a poor, lone woman like me."

"But I don't bring up my sons to do so. If I did, I shouldn't be here now. I am willing to bear my part of the blame, Mrs.

Gregson, but to say I bring my sons up to wickedness, is to lay on me more than my share. Come here, Ranald."

I obeyed with bowed head and shame-stricken heart, for I saw what wrong I had done my father. Although few would be so unjust to him as this old woman, many would yet blame the best man in the world for the wrongs of his children. When I stood by my father's side, the old woman just lifted her head once to cast on me a scowling look, and then went on rocking.

"Now, my boy," said my father, "tell Mrs. Gregson why you have come here tonight."

It was a dreadful effort to make myself speak. It was like resisting a dumb spirit and forcing the words from my lips. But I did not hesitate a moment—I dared not, for hesitation would be defeat. When now I see a child who will not say the words required of him, I feel again just as I felt then, and think how difficult it is for him to do what he is told. But oh, how I wish he would do it, that he might be a conqueror! For I know that if he will not make the effort, it will grow more and more difficult for him to make any effort.

"I came, Mrs. Gregson," I faltered, "to tell you that I am very sorry I behaved so ill to you."

"Yes, indeed," she returned. "How would you like anyone to come and serve you so in your grand house? But a poor, lone widow woman like me is nothing to be thought of. Oh no, not at all!"

"I am ashamed of myself," I said, forcing my confession upon her.

"So you ought to be all the days of your life. You deserve to be drummed out of the town for a minister's son that you are! Hoo!"

"I'll never do it again, Mrs. Gregson."

"You'd better not—or you shall hear of it, if there's a sheriff in the county. To insult honest people after that fashion!"

I drew back, more than ever conscious of the wrong I had done in rousing such unforgiving fierceness in her heart.

My father spoke. "Shall I tell you, Mrs. Gregson, what made the boy sorry, and made him willing to come and tell you all about it?"

"Oh, I've friends after all. The young prodigal!"

"You are coming pretty near it, Mrs. Gregson," said my father, "but you haven't touched it quite. It was a friend of yours that spoke to my boy and made him very unhappy about what he had done, telling him over and over again what a shame it was, and how wicked he was. Do you know what friend it was?"

"Perhaps I do, and perhaps I don't. I can guess."

"It was the best friend you ever had or ever will have. It was God Himself talking in my poor boy's heart, who would not heed what He said all day. But this evening we were reading how the prodigal son went back to his father, and how the father forgave him. Ranald couldn't stand it any longer, and came and told me all about it."

"It wasn't you he had to go to. It wasn't you he smoked to death—was it now? It was easy to go to you."

"Not so easy perhaps. But he has come to you now."

"Come when you made him!"

"I didn't make him. He came gladly, for he saw it was all he could do to make up for the wrong he had done."

"A poor amends!" I heard her grumble, but my father took no notice.

"And you know, Mrs. Gregson," he went on, "when the prodigal son did go back to his father, his father forgave him at once."

"Easy enough! He was his father, and fathers *always* side with their sons."

"Yes, that is true," my father said. "And what God does Himself, He always wants His sons and daughters to do. So He tells us that if we don't forgive one another, He will not forgive us. And as we all want to be forgiven, we had better mind what we're told. If you don't forgive this boy, who has done you a great wrong, but is sorry for it, God will not forgive you—and that's a serious affair."

"He's never begged my pardon yet," said the old woman, whose dignity required my utter humiliation.

"I beg your pardon, Mrs. Gregson," I said. "I shall never be rude to you again."

"Very well," she answered, a little mollified at last. "Keep your promise, and we'll say no more about it. It's for your father's sake, mind, that I forgive you."

A smile trembled about my father's lips, but he suppressed it, saying, "Won't you shake hands with him, Mrs. Gregson?"

She held out a poor shriveled hand, which I took very gladly, but it felt like something half dead. But at the same moment, from behind me, another hand—a rough little hand, but warm and firm and all alive—slipped into my left hand. I knew it was Elsie's, and the thought of how I had behaved to her rushed in upon me with a cold misery of shame. I would have knelt at her feet, but I could not speak my sorrow before witnesses. Therefore I kept hold of her hand and led her to the other end of the cottage, for there was a friendly gloom, the only light in the place coming from the glow—not flame—of a fire of peat and bark.

She came readily, whispering before I had time to open my mouth, "I'm sorry Grannie's so hard to make up to."

"I deserve it," I said. "Elsie, I'm a brute. I could knock my head on the wall. Please forgive me."

"It's not me," she answered. "You didn't hurt me. I didn't mind it."

"O Elsie! I struck you with that horrid snowball."

"It was only on the back of my neck. It didn't hurt me much. It only frightened me."

"I didn't know it was you. If I had known, I shouldn't have done it. But it was wicked and contemptible anyhow, to any girl."

I broke down again, half from shame, half from the happiness of having cast my sin from me by confessing it.

Elsie held my hand now. "Never mind, never mind," she said. "You won't do it again."

"I would rather be hanged," I sobbed.

That moment a pair of strong hands caught hold of mine, and the next moment I found myself being hoisted on somebody's back. Then Turkey's voice said, "I'm his horse again, Elsie, and I'll carry him home this very night."

Elsie gave a pleased little laugh, and Turkey bore me to the fireside, where my father was talking away in a low tone to the old woman. I believe he had now turned the tables upon her, and was trying to convince her of her unkind and grumbling ways. But he did not let us hear a word of the reproof.

"Eh, Turkey, my lad! Is that you? I didn't know you were there," he said. I had never before heard my father address him as Turkey. "What are you doing with that great boy upon your back?" he continued.

"I'm going to carry him home, sir."

"Nonsense! He can walk well enough."

Half ashamed, I began to struggle to get down, but Turkey held me tight.

"But you see, sir," said Turkey, "we're friends now. He's done what he could, and I want to do what I can."

"Very well," returned my father, rising. "Come along—it's time we were going."

When Papa bade her good-night, the old woman actually rose and held out her hand to both of us.

No conqueror was ever happier than I, as through the starry night I rode home on Turkey's back. The very stars seemed to rejoice over my head. "There is joy in the presence of the angels of God over one sinner that repents," and I believe they rejoiced then, for if ever I repented in my life I repented then. When I lay down in bed beside Davie, it seemed as if there could be nobody in the world so blessed as I was: I had been forgiven.

Before getting up the next morning I had a rare game with Davie, who shrieked with laughter. The weather was much the same, but its dreariness had vanished. There was a glowing spot in my heart which drove out the cold and glorified the black frost that bound the earth. When I went out before breakfast, the red face of the sun looked through the mist and seemed to know all about it. I was quite as well satisfied as if the sun of my dream had given me a friendly nod of forgiveness.

CHAPTER NINETEEN
A Fall and a Dream

Elsie Duff's father was a farm laborer, with a large family. He was a cottar: of the large farm upon which he worked for yearly wages, he had a little bit of land to cultivate for his own use. His mother-in-law was Grannie Gregson, who was so old that she needed someone to look after her. She had a cottage of her own in the village, and Elsie was sent to be her companion. It was a great trial to her at first, for her own home was a happy one, and she greatly preferred the open fields to the streets of the village. She did not grumble, however, for where is the good of grumbling where duty is plain, or even when a thing cannot be helped?

Elsie found it very lonely though, so her parents sent her little brother Jamie to live with his grannie and go to school. The intention had been that Elsie herself should go to school, but with tending the cow and her grandmother together she had not been able to begin.

Jamie was a poor little white-haired, red-eyed boy who was often teased by the bigger boys at school. On the whole he was rather a favorite, for he looked so pitiful, and took everything so patiently. I was delighted at the chance of showing Elsie Duff some kindness through her brother. I saw one day, before the master arrived, that Jamie was shivering with cold. So I made room for him by the fire—and then found that he had next to nothing upon his little body, and that the soles of his shoes were hanging half off. This in the month of March in the north of Scotland was bad enough, even if he had not had a cough.

My father sent me to tell Mrs. Mitchell to find some old

garments of Allister's for him, but she declared there were none. When I told Turkey this, he looked very grave, but said nothing. My father had me take Jamie to the tailor and shoemaker, and get warm and strong clothes and shoes made for him. I had not seen his sister—to speak to I mean—since that Sunday night.

One Saturday afternoon, as we were playing at hare and hounds, I was running very hard through the village. I set my foot on a loose stone, and had a violent fall. When I got up, I saw Jamie standing concerned by my side. Finding the blood streaming down my face, and realizing that I was near the house where Turkey's mother lived, I crawled there, and up the stairs to her garret. Jamie followed in silence.

Turkey's mother was busy as usual at her wheel, with Elsie standing talking to her, as if she had just run in for a moment and should not sit down. Elsie gave a little cry when she saw me. Turkey's mother made me take her chair while she hastened to get some water. I grew faint, and passed out. When I came to, I was leaning against Elsie, whose face was as white as a sheet.

Turkey's mother gave me water and tied up my head and persuaded me to lie down a while. A sense of blissful repose pervaded me when I stretched myself on the quilt-covered bed. A single ray of sunlight fell on the floor from the little window in the roof. The hum of the spinning wheel sounded sleepy in my ears. To my half-closed eyes, the sloping ray of light became a Jacob's ladder, crowded with ascending and descending angels, and I thought it was the same ladder I saw in my dreams. Drowsy delight possessed me, and the little garret began to gather about it the hues of Paradise.

Then Elsie began to sing, clear and melodious as a brook, and before she ceased, I was indeed in a kind of paradise. Her voice went through every corner of my brain, singing in all its chambers, and put me to sleep.

I was dreaming of a summer evening. The sun was of a tremendous size, and of a splendid rose-color. He was resting with his lower edge on the horizon, and dared go no farther, because all the flowers would sing instead of giving out their proper scents. If he left them, he feared utter anarchy in his kingdom before he returned in the morning.

Meanwhile, Jamie was sent to tell my father what had happened. Jamie gave the message to Mrs. Mitchell—who, full of her own importance, set out to see how much was the matter. I awoke and saw her ugly face bending over me, pushing me, and calling me to wake up. The moment I saw her I shut my eyes tight and pretended to be fast asleep, hoping that she would go away and leave me with my friends.

"Do let him have his sleep out, Mrs. Mitchell," said Turkey's mother.

"You've let him sleep too long already," she answered ungraciously. "He'll do all he can, waking or sleeping, to make himself troublesome. He's a ne'er-do-well, Ranald. Little good will ever come of him."

"You're wrong there, Mrs. Mitchell," said Elsie. It required a good deal of courage to stand up against an older woman, the housekeeper to the minister. "Ranald is a good boy."

"How dare you say so, when he served your poor old grandmother such a wicked trick? It's little the children care for their parents nowadays. Don't speak to me!"

"No, Elsie, don't speak to her," said another voice, accompanied by a creaking of a door and a heavy step, "or you'll have the worst of it. Leave her to me. Ranald was at least very sorry for it afterward, Mrs. Mitchell, and begged Grannie's pardon—and that's something *you* never did in your life."

"I've had no occasion, Turkey, so hold your tongue."

"Don't you call me *Turkey!* I was christened as well as you."

"And what are *you* to speak to me like that? Go home to your cows. I dare say they're standing supperless in their stalls while you're gadding about. I'll call you *Turkey* as long as I please."

"Very well, Kelpie—that's the name you're known by,

though perhaps no one has been polite enough to use it to your face, for you're a great woman, no doubt. I give you warning that I know you. When you're found out, don't say I didn't give you a chance beforehand."

"You impudent beggar!" cried Mrs. Mitchell. "And you're all one pack," she added, looking around on the two others. "Get up, Ranald, and come home with me. What are you lying shamming there for?"

She approached the bed, but Turkey stepped in front of her. She dared not lay hands upon the great strong lad, so she turned in a rage and stalked out of the room saying, "Mr. Bannerman shall hear of this!"

"Then it'll be *both* sides of it, Mrs. Mitchell," I cried from the bed, but she vanished without reply.

Once more Turkey carried me home on his back. I told my father the whole occurrence. He examined the cut and plastered it up for me, saying he would go and thank Turkey's mother at once. I thought more of Elsie's wonderful singing, which had put me to sleep and given me the strange lovely dream.

Although I never dared go near her grandmother's house alone, I yet got many a glimpse of Elsie. Sometimes I went with Turkey to his mother's in the evening, and Elsie was sure to be there, and we all spent a very happy hour or two together. Sometimes she would sing, and sometimes I would read to them out of Milton. Although there was much of Milton I could not understand, he affected every one of us. The best influences which bear upon us are of this vague sort—powerful upon the heart and conscience, although undefined to the intellect.

CHAPTER TWENTY
The Bees' Nest

It was twelve o'clock on a delicious Saturday in the height of summer, and we poured out of school with the gladness of a holiday in our hearts. I sauntered home full of the summer sun, and the summer wind, and the summer scents which filled the air. I often sat on the earthen walls which divided the fields from the road, and basked in the heat. These walls were covered with grass and moss and a yellow feathery flower. Great bumblebees haunted the walls, and were poking about in them constantly.

It was almost dinnertime before I reached home, and I hurried over my food to get out again into the broad sunlight. I was leaning in utter idleness over our front gate, when a troop of children passed with little baskets and tin pails in their hands, and among them was Jamie Duff. It was not necessary to ask him where he was going.

About a mile from our house was a hill famous for its bilberries. In summer it was of course the haunt of children gathering its bilberries. Jamie shyly suggested whether I would not join them, but they were all too much younger than myself, and besides I felt drawn to seek Turkey—that is, when I should get quite tired of doing nothing.

The little troop had streamed on, and I was suddenly startled by a sound beside me. I saw Eppie—an old woman, bent nearly double within an old gray cloak despite the heat. She leaned on a stick, and carried a bag like a pillowcase in her hand. She was making her rounds for her weekly dole of a handful of oatmeal. I knew her very well, and a kindly greeting passed between us.

She passed in at our gate and went as usual to the kitchen door, while I stood drowsily contemplating the green growing crops in the valley. The day had grown as sleepy as myself. There were no noises except the hum of the unseen insects, and the distant rush of the water over the dams.

In a few minutes Eppie approached me again. She was an honest and worthy soul, and very civil in her manners. Therefore I was surprised to hear her muttering to herself. Very angry and vexed, she stopped muttering when she saw me watching, and walked on in silence. I put my hand in my pocket, and pulled out a halfpenny my father had given me that morning—very few of which came my way—and offered it to her. She took it with a half-ashamed glance, a curtsy, and a murmured blessing. She looked as if she was about to say something else, but changed her mind. She only added another grateful word, and hobbled away. I concluded that the Kelpie had been rude to her. Then I forgot her, and fell a-dreaming again. Finally tired of doing nothing, I set out to seek Turkey.

I visited Kirsty to find out where Turkey was. I told her about Eppie, and her altered looks when she came out of the house. Kirsty compressed her lips, nodded her head, looked serious, and made no reply. Thinking this was strange, I resolved to tell Turkey, which otherwise I might not have done. Having learned that he was close by the scene of our adventure with Wandering Willie, I set out to find him.

I soon came in sight of the cattle feeding, but did not see Turkey. I glimpsed old Mrs. Gregson's cow quietly feeding off the top of the wall from the other side, while my father's cows were busy in the short clover inside. And Elsie Duff was inside the wall, seated on a stone which Turkey had no doubt dragged there for her. Elsie was as usual busy with her knitting. And now I caught sight of Turkey, running from a neighboring cottage with a spade over his shoulder. Elsie had been minding the cows for him.

"What's ado, Turkey?" I cried.

"Such a wild bees' nest! I was just thinking I would run

and fetch you. Elsie and I have been watching them for the last half-hour. Such a lot of bees! There's a store of honey in *there.* You must keep a sharp lookout though, Ranald. They'll be mad enough, and you must keep them off with your cap."

He took off his own cap and gave it to Elsie, saying, "Here, Elsie, you must look out, and keep the bees off you. A sting is no joke—I've had three myself."

"But what are *you* to do, Turkey?" asked Elsie, with an anxious face.

"Oh, Ranald will keep them off of me and himself too. I must dig away, and get at the honey."

Turkey manfully approached the wall. In the midst of the grass and moss was one little hole, through which the bees kept going and coming. Turkey struck his spade with firm foot into the wall. What bees were in came rushing out in fear and rage, and I had to work to keep them off our bare heads with my cap. Elsie, staying still at a little distance, was less the object of their resentment. In a few moments Turkey reached the store and began to dig about it as coolly as if he had been gardening. All the defense he left to me, and I thought mine the harder work of the two.

But now Turkey stooped to the nest, cleared away the earth with his hands, and with much care drew out a great piece of honeycomb. Its surface was even and yellow, its cells full to the brim. Turkey picked away some bits of adhering mold before he presented it to Elsie. She sat on her stone like a patient, contented queen, waiting for what her subjects would bring her.

"O Turkey! What a piece!" Elsie said as she took it, and opened her pretty mouth and white teeth to have a bite of the treasure.

"Now, Ranald," said Turkey, "we must finish the job before we have any ourselves."

He went on carefully removing the honey and piling it on the bank. Then he filled up the hole, and beat the earth down hard. Last of all, he replaced the sod, with the grass and flowers still growing upon it. Then he divided what remained of the honey.

"There's a piece for Allister and Davie," he said, "and here's a piece for you, and this for me. Elsie can take the rest home for herself and Jamie."

We sat and ate our shares, and chatted away. Turkey and I got up every now and then to look after the cattle, and Elsie too had sometimes to follow her cow. But there was plenty of time between, and Elsie sung us two or three songs. Turkey told us one or two stories out of his history books, and I read them a story as well. And so the hot sun went down in the glowing west, and threw longer and longer shadows eastward.

It was time for the cattle, Elsie's cow included, to go home. But just then a little girl came flying to us across the field. She lived nearby, and was one of the little troop that had gone to gather bilberries.

"Elsie! Elsie!" she cried. "John Adam has taken Jamie! Jamie fell, and John got him!"

Elsie looked frightened, but Turkey laughed, saying, "Never mind, Elsie. John is better than he looks. He won't do Jamie the least harm—but he must mind his business."

The hill was covered with a young plantation of firs. It was among their small stems that the coveted bilberries grew, in company with cranberries and crowberries and dwarf junipers. The children of the village who came to the place were no doubt careless of the young trees, and might sometimes do them damage. The keeper, John Adam, whose business it was to look after the trees, waged war upon these invaders—and in their eyes Adam was a terrible man. He was very long and very lean, with a flattish nose and a rather ill-tempered mouth, while his face was dead white and much pitted with smallpox. He wore corduroy breeches, a blue coat, and a striped nightcap.

He could not run very fast, and if the children had a head start, and did not choose the wrong direction, they were pretty sure to get away. Jamie Duff, the most harmless and conscientious creature, who would not have injured a young fir upon any temptation, did take a wrong direction, caught his foot in a hole, and fell into a furze bush. He was seized by Adam, lifted high into the air, and borne off as a warning to the rest.

But John Adam was not so frightful to Turkey, who soon calmed Elsie. He assured her that he would walk over to Adam's house and try to get Jamie off. Elsie set off home with her cow, sad but hopeful. I helped Turkey fasten up the cows, and shared his hasty supper of potatoes and oatcake and milk. Then we set out for the home of the fearful ogre.

CHAPTER TWENTY-ONE

Vain Intercession

John Adam had a small farm of his own at the foot of the hill in his charge. It was a poor little place, with a very low thatched cottage for the dwelling. His sister kept house for him. When we approached it there was no one to be seen, so we walked to the door along a rough pavement of round stones. I peeped in at the little window as we passed. There, to my astonishment, I saw Jamie Duff—looking very happy, and in the act of lifting a spoon to his mouth. But when Turkey lifted the latch and we walked in, there were the awful John and his sister seated at the table, while poor Jamie was in a corner with no basin in his hand, and a face that looked dismal and dreary enough. I fancied Turkey was laughing in his sleeve, and felt mildly indignant with him— for Elsie's sake more than for Jamie's.

"Come in," said Adam. "Oh, it's you, Turkey! Come in and take a spoon."

"No, thank you," said Turkey. "I have had my supper. I only came to see about that young rascal there."

"Ah! You see him! There he is!" said Adam, looking toward me with an awful expression in his dead brown eyes. "Starving. No home and no supper for him! He'll have to sleep in the hayloft with the rats, and mice, and stray cats."

Jamie put his shirtcuffs to his eyes. His fate was full of horrors. But again I thought I saw Turkey laughing in his sleeve.

"His sister is very anxious about him, Mr. Adam," he said. "Couldn't you let him off this once?"

"On no account. The duke gives me charge of the forest,

and I have to look after it. And if wicked boys will break down the trees—"

"I only pulled down the bilberries," interposed Jamie, in a whine which went off in a howl.

"James Duff!" said Adam, with awful authority. "I myself saw you tumble over a young larch not two feet high."

"The worse for me!" sobbed Jamie.

"Tut! Tut! Mr. Adam! The larch wasn't a baby," said Turkey. "Let Jamie go. He couldn't help it, you see."

"It *was* a baby, and it *is* a baby," said Adam, with a solitary twinkle in the determined dead brown of his eyes. "And I'll have no intercession here. Transgressors must be prosecuted. He shan't get out of this before church-time tomorrow morning. We must make some examples, you see. Jamie's just as bad as the rest, else how did he come to be there tumbling over my babies? Answer me that, Master Bannerman." He turned and fixed his awful gaze upon me, and my eyes sank before his.

"Example, Master Bannerman, is everything!" He brought down his fist on the table with such a bang that poor Jamie almost fell off the stool.

"But let him off this once," pleaded Turkey, "and I'll be the surety for him that he'll never do it again."

"Oh, I'm not afraid of him," returned the keeper. "But will you be surety for the fifty boys that'll only make game of me if I don't make an example of him? I'm in luck to have caught him. No, Turkey, it won't do. I'm sorry for his father and mother and sister, for they're all very good people, but I must make an example of him."

"Well, you won't be over hard upon him, will you now?" said Turkey.

"I won't pull his skin *quite* over his ears," said Adam, "but that's all the promise you'll get from me."

I suspected that the keeper's ferocity was a sham, and that he was not such an ogre as I had considered him. Still, the prospect of poor little Jamie spending the night alone in the loft among the cats and rats was dreadful. There seemed to be no help, however, especially when Turkey rose to say good-night. I was not well pleased with Turkey's coolness. I thought he had not done his best.

"Poor Elsie!" I said, when we got to the road. "She'll be miserable about Jamie."

"Oh, no," returned Turkey. "I'll go straight over and tell her. No harm will come to Jamie. John Adam's bark is a good deal worse than his bite."

We walked through the glimmering dusk back to the manse. Turkey left me at the gate and strode on toward the village. I turned in, revolving a new scheme in my brain. For the first time a sense of rivalry with Turkey awoke in my bosom. He did everything for Elsie Duff, and I did nothing. For her he had robbed the bees' nest that very day, and I had but partaken of the spoil. Nay, he had been stung in her service, for with all my care he had received a bad sting on the back of his neck. Now he was going to comfort her about her brother whom he had failed to rescue. But what if I should succeed where he had failed, and carry the poor boy home in triumph!

As we left the keeper's yard, Turkey had pointed out to me the loft in which Jamie would have to sleep. It was over the cart shed, and its approach was a ladder. But for the reported rats, it would have been no hardship to sleep there. But I knew that Jamie was a very timid boy, and that I myself would have lain in horror all the night. Therefore I had been turning over in my mind what I could do to release him. But whatever I did must be unaided, for I could not reckon upon Turkey, nor indeed was it in my heart to share with him the honor of the planned rescue.

CHAPTER TWENTY-TWO
Knight-Errantry

My father never objected now to my riding his little mare Missy. Indeed, I took her out for a trot and a gallop as often as I pleased.

As soon as prayers and supper were over—about ten o'clock—I crept out of the house away to the stable. It was a lovely night. A kind of gray peace filled the earth and air and sky. It was not dark, although rather cloudy; only a dim dusk, like a vapor of darkness, floated around everything. I was fond of being out at night, but I had never before contemplated going so far alone. I should not, however, feel alone with Missy under me.

I opened the door of the stable, for I knew where the key lay. It was very dark, but I felt my way through, talking all the time so that the horses might not be startled. I took care, however, to speak in a low tone so that Andrew, the man who slept next to the stable, might not hear. I soon had the bridle upon Missy, but did not take time to put on the saddle. I led her out, mounted with the help of a stone at the stable door, and rode away. She had scarcely been out all day, and was in the mood for a ride.

I had not gone far before the extreme stillness of the night began to sink into my soul and make me quiet. Everything seemed thinking about me, but nothing would tell me what it thought. Not feeling, however, that I was doing wrong, I was only awed, not frightened of the stillness. I made Missy slacken her speed, and rode on more gently, in better harmony with the night. Not a sound broke the silence except the rough cry of the land rail from the fields and the clatter of Missy's feet. I did not like the noise she made, and got upon grass, for here there was no fence.

But the moment she felt the soft grass, off she galloped. She tore away over the field in quite a new direction at full speed. Frightened, I pulled hard at the reins, but without avail. We galloped down a steep hill, and I began to guess where Missy was carrying me. We were approaching the scene of my adventure with Wandering Willie. The thought was horrible. Besides, if Missy should get into the bog! But she knew better than that, wild as her mood was. She galloped past the bog, dropped into a canter, and then stood stock-still.

Missy had stopped before a half-ruined cottage, occupied by an old woman whom I dimly recalled having once gone with my father to see. Her name was Betty, and she was still alive, though very old and bedridden. I remembered that from the top of her wooden bed hung a rope for her to pull herself up by when she wanted to turn, for she was very rheumatic, and this rope had filled me with horror.

The cottage had once been a smithy, and the bellows had been left in its old place. The huge structure of leather and wood, with the great iron nose projecting from its contracting cheeks, stood at the head of the old woman's bed, so capable yet so useless. I vaguely suspected that the old woman was a bit of a witch. I had a doubtful memory that she had been seen when a frightful storm was raging, blowing away at that very bellows as hard as she could work the lever, so that there was almost as great a storm of wind in her little room as there was outside of it. At any rate, the poor woman had been a little out of her mind for many years—and no wonder, for she was nearly a hundred, they said. Neither is it any wonder that when Missy stopped there so suddenly, that I should feel very strange indeed.

My skin began to creep all over me. An ancient elder tree grew at one end of the cottage, and I heard the lonely sigh of a little breeze wander through its branches. The next instant a frightful sound from within the cottage broke the night air in a universal shriek. Missy plunged, turned around on her hind legs, and tore from the place. I very nearly lost my seat, but terror made me cling to my only companion as she flew home. It did not take her a minute to reach the stable door. It was mortifying to find myself there instead of under John Adam's hayloft. But I did not think of that for a while. Shaken with terror, and afraid to dismount and be on the ground, I called to Andrew.

In a few awful minutes—for who could tell what might be following me up from the hollow?—Andrew appeared half-dressed, and not in the best of tempers. He remarked that it was an odd thing to go out riding when honest people were in their beds. I told him the whole story, what I had intended and how I had been frustrated. He listened, scratched his head, and said someone ought to see to the old woman. He turned in to put on the rest of his clothes.

"You had better go home to bed, Ranald," he said.

"Won't you be frightened, Andrew?" I asked.

"Why should I be frightened? It's all waste to be frightened before you know whether the thing is worth it."

My courage had been reviving fast in the warm presence of a human being. To go home having done nothing for Jamie, and therefore nothing for Elsie, was too mortifying. Yet suppose the something which gave that fearful cry in the cottage should be out roaming the fields and looking for me! I remained where I was till Andrew came out again, and as I sat still on Missy's back, my courage gradually rose. Nothing increases terror so much as running away. I asked Andrew, "What do you think it could be?"

"How should I tell?" he returned. "She has a very odd rooster that always roosts on the top of her bed, and crows like no cock I ever heard. Or it might be Wandering Willie—he goes to see her sometimes, and the demented creature might strike up his pipes at any unearthly hour."

I was not satisfied with either suggestion, but the terrible sound might have been anything. I begged Andrew to put the saddle on for me, as I should then have more command of Missy. He did so, and I buckled on an old rusty spur. Thus armed, and mounted with my feet in stirrups, and therefore a good pull on Missy's mouth, I found my courage once more equal to the task.

Andrew and I parted at right angles—he across the field to the cottage, and I along the road to John Adam's farm.

CHAPTER TWENTY-THREE
Failure

It must have been now about eleven. The clouds had cleared off, and the night had changed from brown and gray to blue sparkling with gold. I had not ridden far from the stable before I again found myself very much alone and unprotected, with only the wide, silent fields about me, and the wider and more silent sky over my head. The fear began to return, and I would fancy there was something strange creeping along every ditch—something shapeless, but with a terrible cry in it. Next I would think I saw something—now like a creature on all fours, now like a man—coming rapidly toward me across the field. But it always vanished.

The faster I rode, the more frightened I became, for my speed drew the terrors after me. So I changed my plan, and drew rein and went slower. I threw defiance to the fear—and it abated. Fear is a worse thing than danger.

We had to pass the pool where Turkey and I had had our adventure with Bogbonny's bull. That story was now far off in the past, but I did not relish the dull shine of the water in the hollow. Somehow I was lifted above the ordinary level of fear by being upon Missy's back, and we passed by. I think many men draw their courage from their horses.

We came in sight of John Adam's farm, and just at that moment the moon peeped from behind a hill, throwing shadows as long as the setting sun, but in the other direction. I rode quietly up to the back of the yard where the ricks stood, got off Missy and fastened the bridle to the gate. I walked across to the cart shed, where the moon was shining upon the ladder leading up to the loft. I climbed the ladder and unfastened the door. When I opened it, the moonlight got in before me, and poured upon the straw in the farthest corner, where Jamie was lying asleep with a rug over him. I crossed the floor, knelt down beside him, and tried to wake him. This was not so easy, for he was far too sound asleep to be troubled even by the rats. Sleep is an armor—a castle—against many enemies.

I lifted one of his hands, and found a cord tied to his wrist. Indignant, I gave the cord a great tug of anger, pulled out my knife, and cut it. Then I hauled Jamie up, half-awake at last. He stared with fright first, and then began to cry, then stopped crying but not staring. His eyes seemed to have nothing better than moonlight in them.

"Come along, Jamie," I said. "I've come to take you home."

"I don't want to go home," said Jamie. "I want to go to sleep again."

"That's very ungrateful of you, Jamie," I said, full of my own importance, "when I've come so far, and all at night too, to set you free."

"I'm free enough," said Jamie. "I had a great deal better supper than I should have had at home. I don't want to go before the morning." And he began to whimper again.

"Do you call this free?" I said, holding up his wrist where the remnant of the cord was hanging.

"Oh!" said Jamie. "That's only—"

Just then the moonlight in the loft was darkened. In the doorway stood a great tall woman, with the moon behind her. I thought at first it was the Kelpie come after me; my heart gave a great jump up, but I swallowed it down. It was John Adam's sister, the great, grim, gaunt woman I had seen at the table at supper. I had myself raised the apparition, for the cord which was tied to Jamie's wrist, instead of being meant to keep him a prisoner, was a device of her kindness to keep him from being too frightened. The other end had been tied to her wrist, that if anything happened he might pull her, and then she would come to him.

"What's the matter, Jamie Duff?" she said in a gruff voice as she advanced along the stream of moonlight.

I stood up bravely. "It's only me, Miss Adam."

"And who are you?" she returned.

"Ranald Bannerman," I answered.

"Oh!" she said in a puzzled tone. "What are you doing here at this time of the night?"

"I came to take Jamie home, but he won't go."

"You're a silly boy to think my brother would do him any harm," she returned. "You're comfortable enough, aren't you, Jamie?"

"Yes, thank you, ma'am, quite comfortable," said Jamie, now wide awake. "But please, ma'am, Ranald didn't mean any harm."

"He's a housebreaker, though," she rejoined with a grim chuckle, "and he'd better go home again. If John should come out, I don't exactly know what might happen. Or perhaps he'd like to stop and keep you company."

"No, thank you, Miss Adam," I said. "I will go home."

"Come along, then, and let me shut the door after you."

Somewhat nettled with Jamie Duff's indifference to my well-meant exertions on his behalf, I followed her without even bidding him good-night.

"Oh, you've got Missy, have you?" she said, spying the mare. "Would you like a drink of milk or a piece of oatcake before you go?"

"No, thank you," I said. "I shall be glad to go to bed."

"I should think so," she answered. "Jamie is quite comfortable, I assure you, and I'll take care he's in time for the service at church tomorrow. There's no harm in *him,* poor thing!"

She undid the bridle for me, helped me to mount in the kindest way, and bade me good-night. I went home at a good gallop, took off the saddle and bridle and laid them in a cart in the shed, turned Missy loose into the stable, shut the door, and ran across the field to the manse, desiring nothing but bed.

But when I neared the house from the back, I saw a figure entering the gate from the front: it was the Kelpie. She entered, and closed the door behind her very softly. Afraid of being locked out, I hastened after her. The door was already fastened, so I called through the keyhole. She gave a cry of alarm, but opened the door, looking pale and frightened.

"What are you doing out-of-doors at this time of night?" she asked, but with a trembling voice.

"What were *you* doing out yourself?"

"Looking for you, of course."

"That's why you locked the door, I suppose—to keep me out."

She had no answer ready, but looked as if she would have struck me. "I shall let your father know of your goings on," she said, recovering herself a little.

"You need not take the trouble. I shall tell him myself at breakfast tomorrow morning. I have nothing to hide. You had better tell him too."

I did not believe she had been out to look for me, but I did think she had locked the door to annoy me, and I wanted to take my revenge in rudeness. For doors were seldom locked in the summer nights in that part of the country. She made no reply, but turned and left me, not even shutting the door. I closed it, and went to bed weary enough.

CHAPTER TWENTY-FOUR

Turkey Plots

The next day at breakfast, I told my father all the previous day's adventures. Never since he had so kindly rescued me from the misery of wickedness had I concealed anything from him. He, on his part, while he gave us every freedom, expected us to speak frankly concerning our doings. To have been unwilling to let him know any of our proceedings would have simply argued that we already disapproved of them. In this way he ever lifted us up toward his own higher level.

This was Sunday, but he was not so strict in his ideas concerning the day as most of his parishioners. So long as we were sedate and orderly, and neither talked nor laughed too loud, he seldom interfered with our behavior. He did not require or expect us to care about religious things as much as he did: we could not yet know as he did what they really were. Yet he thought that to order our ways was our best preparation for receiving higher instruction afterward.

He listened attentively to my story, seemed puzzled at the cry I heard from the cottage, said nothing could have gone very wrong, or we should have heard of it now from Andrew. He laughed over the apparition of Miss Adam, and my failure in rescuing Jamie Duff. He said, however, that I had no right to interfere with constituted authority—that John Adam was put there to protect the trees, that Jamie was certainly trespassing, and that I ought to have been satisfied with Turkey's way of looking at the matter.

I saw that my father was right. Further reflection convinced me that, although my conduct had a root in my regard for Jamie Duff, it had a deeper root in my regard for his sister, and one yet deeper in my regard for myself—for had I not longed to show off in her eyes? I suspect almost all silly actions have their root in selfishness, whether it takes the form of vanity, conceit, greed, or ambition.

While I was telling my tale, Mrs. Mitchell kept coming into the room and lingering. I said nothing about her, for I saw no occasion. But she was afraid I would, and wished to be at hand to defend herself.

When we came out, I saw Andrew. He told me he had found all perfectly quiet at the cottage, except for the old woman's troublesome cough, which gave proof that she was alive, and as well as usual. He suggested that the noise was all a fancy of mine—at which I was duly indignant, and desired to know if it was also Missy's fancy that made her go off like a mad creature. He then returned to his former idea of the cock, and as this did not insult my dignity, I let it pass. I, however, leaned to the notion of Wandering Willie's pipes.

On the following Wednesday we had a half holiday, and before dinner I went to find Turkey at the farm. He met me in the yard, and took me into the barn.

"I want to speak to you, Ranald," he said. "I can't bear that the master should have bad people about him."

"What do you mean, Turkey?" I responded.

"I mean the Kelpie."

"She's a nasty thing, I know," I answered. "But my father considers her a faithful servant."

"That's just it. She is *not* faithful. I've suspected her for a long time. She's so rough and ill-tempered that she looks honest, but I shall be able to show her up yet. You wouldn't call it honest to cheat the poor, would you?"

"I should think not. But what do you mean?"

"There must have been something to put old Eppie in such an ill-temper on Saturday, don't you think?"

"I suppose she had a sting from the Kelpie's tongue."

"No, Ranald, that's not it. I had heard whispers going about, and last Saturday, after we came home from John

Adam's, and after I had told Elsie about Jamie, I ran up to see old Eppie. You would have gotten nothing out of her, but she told me all about it."

"Everybody tells you everything, Turkey!"

"No, Ranald, I'm not such a gossip as that. But when you have a chance, you ought to set right whatever you can. Right's the only thing, Ranald."

"But aren't you afraid they'll call you a meddler, Turkey? Not that *I* think so, for I'm sure if you do anything *against* anybody, it's *for* some other body."

"That would be no justification if I wasn't in the right," said Turkey. "But I'm willing to bear any blame that comes of it. And I wouldn't meddle for anybody that could take care of himself. But neither old Eppie nor your father can do that: the one's too poor, and the other too good. Your father believes in everybody. *I* wouldn't have kept the Kelpie in *my* house half the time."

"But what's the Kelpie been doing to old Eppie?"

"First of all, Eppie has been playing her a trick."

"Then she mustn't complain."

"Eppie's was a lawful trick, though. There has been for some time a growing conviction among the poor folk that the Kelpie never gives them an honest handful of meal when they make their rounds. But it was hard to prove, so the old women laid their heads together, and resolved that some of them should go with empty bags. Every one of those found a full handful at the bottom. Still, they were not satisfied. So Eppie went with something at the bottom of her bag to look like a quantity of meal already gathered. The moment the door was closed behind her—that was last Saturday—she peeped into the bag. Not one grain of meal was there. That was why she passed you muttering to herself and looking so angry.

"Now it will never do that the manse, of all places, should be the one where the poor people are cheated of their dues. But we must have yet better proof than this before we can say anything."

"Why does she do it, Turkey?" I asked. "It's not for the sake of saving my father's meal, I should think."

"No, she does something with it, and, I suppose, flatters herself that she's not stealing—only saving it off the poor, and so making a right to it for herself. I can't help thinking that her being out that same night had something to do with it. Did you ever know her to go see old Betty?"

"No, she doesn't like her. I know that."

"I'm not so sure. She pretends perhaps. But we'll have a try. I think I can outwit her. She's fair game, you know."

"How? What? Do tell me, Turkey!" I cried eagerly.

"Not today. I will tell you by and by."

He got up and went about his work.

CHAPTER TWENTY-FIVE

Old John Jamieson

As I returned to the house, I met my father.

"Well, Ranald, what are you about?" he asked, in his usual gentle tone.

"Nothing in particular, Father," I answered.

"Well, I'm going to see old John Jamieson. I don't think you know him, for he has not been able to come to church for a long time. They tell me he is dying. Would you like to go with me?"

"Yes, Father. But won't you take Missy?"

"Not if you will walk with me. It's only three miles."

"Very well, Father. I should like to go with you."

My father talked about various things on the way. I remember in particular some remarks he made about Virgil,* for I had just begun the *Aeneid.* He told me I must scan every line until I could make it sound like poetry, else I should neither enjoy it properly, nor be fair to the author. Then he repeated some lines from Milton, saying them first as prose, and then as they ought to be sounded, making me mark the difference. Next he did the same with the opening lines of Virgil's great poem, and made me feel the difference there.

"The sound is the shape of it, Ranald," he said, "for a poem is all for the ear and not for the eye. The eye sees only the sense of it, while the ear sees the shape of it. To judge poetry without heeding the sound of it is nearly as bad as judging a rose by smelling it with your eyes shut. The sound, besides being a beautiful thing in itself, has a sense in it which helps the other out. A good psalm tune helps you to see how beautiful the psalm is. Every poem carries its own tune in its own heart, and to read it aloud is the only way to bring out its tune."

I liked Virgil much better after this, and always tried to get at the tune of it and of every other poem I read.

"The right way of anything," said my father, "may be called the tune of it. We have to find out the tune of our own lives. Some people don't seem ever to find it out, and so their lives are broken and uncomfortable—full of ups and downs and disappointments, and never going as they were meant to go."

"But what is the right tune of a body's life, Father?"

"The will of God, my boy."

"But how is a person to know that?"

"By trying to do what he knows of it already. Everybody has a different kind of tune in his life, and no one can find out another's tune for him, though he *may* help him to find it for himself."

"But aren't we to read the Bible, Father?"

"Yes, if it's in order to obey it. To read the Bible thinking to please God by the mere reading of it, is to think like a heathen."

"And aren't we to say our prayers?"

"We are to ask God for what we want. If we don't want a thing, we are only acting like pagans to speak as if we did, and call it prayer, and think we are pleasing Him."

I was silent. My father resumed, "I fancy the old man we are going to see found the tune of *his* life long ago."

"Is he a very wise man then, Father?"

"That depends on what you mean by *wise. I* should call him a wise man, for to find out that tune is the truest wisdom. But he's not a learned man at all. I doubt if he ever read a book about the Bible, except perhaps *Pilgrim's Progress.* I believe he has always been very fond of that. *You* like that, don't you, Ranald?"

"I've read it a good many times, Father. But I was a little tired of it before I got through it last time."

"But you did read it through the last time?"

"Oh, yes, Father. I never like to leave the loose end of a thing hanging about."

"That's right, my boy, that's right. Well, I think you'd better not open that book again for a long time—say twenty years at least. It's a great deal too good a book to let yourself get tired of. By that time I trust you will be able to understand it a great deal better."

I felt sorry that I was not to look at *Pilgrim's Progress* for twenty years, but I am very glad of it now.

"We must not spoil good books by reading them too much," my father added. "It is often better to think about them than to read them, and it is best never to do either when we are tired of them. We should get tired of the beautiful sunlight itself if God did not send it away every night. We're not even fit to have moonlight always. The moon is buried in the darkness every month. And because we can bear nothing for any length of time together, we are sent to sleep every night, so that we may begin fresh again in the morning."

"I see, Father, I see," I answered.

We talked on until we came to John Jamieson's cottage. What a poor little place it was—built of clay which had hardened in the sun till it was just one brick! But it was a better place to live in than it looked, for no wind could come through the walls. It stood on the side of a healthy hill, which rose up steep behind it and sheltered it from the north. A low wall of loose stones enclosed a small garden, reclaimed from the hill, where grew some greens and cabbages and potatoes, with a flower here and there between. A little brook went cantering down the hill close to the end of the cottage, singing merrily.

My father had to bend his head low to enter the cottage. An old woman, the sick man's wife, rose from the side of the chimney to greet us. My father asked how John was.

"Wearing away," she said, "but he'll be glad to see you."

We turned, and I saw a small, withered head and a withered hand, large and bony. The old man lay in a bed closed in with boards, so that very little light fell upon him, but his hair glistened silvery through the gloom. My father drew a chair beside him. John looked up, and seeing who it was, feebly held out his hand. My father took it and stroked it.

"Well, John, my man, you've had a hard life of it."

"No harder than I could bear," said John.

"It's a grand thing to be able to say that," said my father.

"O sir, for that matter, I would go through it all again, if it was His will, and willingly. I have no will but His, sir."

"Well, John, I wish we could all say the same. When a man comes to that, the Lord lets him have what he wants. What do you want now, John?"

"To depart and be with the Lord. It wouldn't be true, sir, to say that I wasn't weary. It seems to me, if it's the Lord's will, I've had enough of this life. Even if death be a very long sleep, as some people say, till the judgment, I think I would rather sleep, for I'm very weary. Only there's the old woman there! I don't like leaving her."

"But you can trust God for her too, can't you?"

"It would be a poor thing if I couldn't, sir."

"Were you ever dreadfully hungry, John?"

"Never longer than I could bear," he answered. "When you think it's the will of God, hunger doesn't get much hold of you, sir."

"You must excuse me, John, for asking so many questions. You know God better than I do, and I want my young man here to know how strong the will of God makes a man, old or young. He needn't care about anything else, need he?"

"There's nothing else to care about, sir. If only the will of God be done, everything's all right, you know. I do believe, sir, that God cares more for me than my old woman herself does, and she's been as good a wife to me as ever was. Young gentleman, you know who says that God numbers the very hairs of our heads? There's not many of mine left to number," he added with a faint smile, "but there's plenty of yours. You mind the will of God, and He'll look after you.

That's the way He divides the business of life."

I saw now that my father's talk as we came had been to prepare me for John Jamieson's words. I did not understand the old man at the time, but his words have often come back to me since, and helped me through pretty severe trials—although, like him, I have never found any of them too hard to bear.

"I have had ten children, sir," the old man went on, "but only three are left alive. There'll be plenty to welcome me home when I go. One's in Canada, and another's in Australia, and they can't come. But Maggie's not far off, and I should like her to see the last of her old father, for I shall be young again by the next time she sees me, please God, sir. He's all in all—isn't He, sir?"

"True, John. If we have God, we have all things, for all things are His and we are His. But we mustn't weary you too much. Thank you for your good advice."

"I beg your pardon, sir—I had no intention of speaking like that. I never could give advice in all my life. I always found it was as much as I could do to take the good advice that was given to me. I should like to be prayed for in church next Sunday, sir, if you please."

"But can't you pray for yourself, John?"

"Yes, sir, but I would like to have some spiritual gift because my friends asked it for me. Let them pray for more faith for me. I want more and more of that, for the more you have, the more you want. Don't you, sir? And I mightn't ask enough for myself, now I'm so old and so tired. I sleep a great deal, sir."

"Don't you think God will give you enough, even if you shouldn't ask for enough?" said my father.

"No doubt of that. But you see I am able to think of it now, and so I must set things going for the time when I shan't be able to think of it."

My father prayed by John's bedside, pulled a parcel or two from his pocket for his wife, and then we walked home together in silence.

CHAPTER TWENTY-SIX

Turkey's Trick

When we came to the farm on our way home, we looked in to see Kirsty, but found the key in the door, indicating that she had gone out. As we left the yard, we saw a strange beggar woman approaching. She had a sack wallet over her shoulder, and walked stooping with her great eyes on the ground, not lifting them to greet us—rare behavior in our parish. My father took no notice, but I could not help turning to look after the woman. To my surprise she stood looking after us, but the moment I turned, she turned also and walked on.

When I looked again she had vanished. Of course she must have gone into the farmyard. Not liking the look of her, and remembering that Kirsty was out, I asked my father whether I had not better see if any of the men were about the stable. He approved, and I ran back to the house. The door was still locked. I called Turkey, and heard his voice in reply from one end of the farthest of the cow-houses. When I had reached it, and told him my story, he threw down his pitchfork, and came with me. We searched all about the place, but could find no sign whatever of the woman.

"Are you sure it wasn't all a fancy of your own, Ranald?" said Turkey.

"Quite sure. Ask my father. She passed as near us as you are to me now."

I heard my father calling, so I ran to him, and told him there was no woman to be seen.

"That's odd," he said. "She must have passed straight through the yard and out the other side before you went in.

Come along, and let us have our tea."

I could not feel quite satisfied about it, but, as there was no other explanation, I convinced myself that my father was right.

The next Saturday evening I was in the nursery with my brothers. It was growing dusk when I heard a knocking. Mrs. Mitchell did not seem to hear it, so I went and opened the door. There was the same beggar woman. Rather frightened, I called Mrs. Mitchell, who appeared with a wooden basin filled with meal. She took a handful as she came in apparent preparation for dropping it, in the customary way, into the woman's bag. The woman never spoke, but closed the mouth of her wallet, and turned away.

Curiosity gave me courage to follow her. She walked with long strides in the direction of the farm, and I kept at a little distance behind her. She made for the yard, but she could not escape me this time. As soon as she entered it, I ran as fast as I could, and just caught sight of her back as she went into one of the cow-houses. I darted after her. She turned round upon me fiercely—but then she held out the open mouth of the bag toward me, and said, "Not one grain, Ranald! Put in your hand and feel!"

It was Turkey! I stared in amazement, unable for a time to get rid of the apparition and see the reality. Turkey burst out laughing at my perplexity.

"Why didn't you tell me before, Turkey?" I asked.

"Because then you would have had to tell your father, and I did not want him to be troubled about it, at least before we got things clear. I always *did* wonder how he could keep such a creature about him."

"He doesn't know her as we do, Turkey."

"No. She never gives him the chance. But now, Ranald, couldn't you manage to find out where she stores the meal she pretends to give away?"

A thought struck me. "I heard Davie the other day asking her why she had two meal tubs. Perhaps that has something to do with it."

"You must find out. Don't ask Davie."

For the first time it occurred to me that the Kelpie had upon that night of the terror been out on business of her own, and had not been looking for me at all.

"Then she was down at old Betty's cottage," said Turkey, when I told him my suspicion, "and Wandering Willie was there too, and Andrew was right about the pipes. Willie hasn't been once to this house since he took Davie, but she has gone to meet him at Betty's. Depend on it, Ranald, he's her brother, or nephew, or something, as I used to say. I do believe she gives him the meal to take home to her family somewhere. Did you ever hear anything about her friends?"

"I never hear her speak of any."

"Then I don't believe they're respectable. But it will be a great trouble to the minister to have to turn her away. I wonder if we couldn't contrive to make her go on her own. I wish we could scare her out of the country. It's not nice for a woman like that to have to do with such innocents as Allister and Davie."

"She's very fond of Davie."

"So she is. That's the only good thing I know of her. But hold your tongue, Ranald, till we find out more."

I soon discovered the second meal tub—small, and carefully stowed away. It was now nearly full, and every day I watched in the hope that when she emptied it, I should be able to find out what she did with the meal. But Turkey's suggestion about frightening her away kept working in my brain.

CHAPTER TWENTY-SEVEN

I Scheme Too

I began a series of persecutions of the Kelpie on my own account. I was doubtful whether Turkey would approve of them, so I did not tell him for some time, though I was anxious to show him that I could do something without him.

There was a closet in the hall, the floor of which was directly over the Kelpie's bed. With a gimlet I bored a hole in the floor, through which I passed a piece of string. I sewed and stuffed a bit of black cloth into something of the shape of a rat. I tied this to the end of the string by the head, and hid it under her bolster.

When she was going to bed, I went to the closet, laid my mouth to the floor, and began squeaking like a rat and scratching with my nails. I tugged at the string, which lifted the bolster a little, and of course out came my rat. I heard her scream, and open the door. I pulled the rat up tight to the ceiling. Then the door of the nursery, where we slept only in the winter, opened and shut, and I concluded she had gone to bed there to avoid the rat. I could hardly sleep for the pleasure at my success.

The next morning, she told my father that she had seen in her bed the biggest rat she ever saw in her life, and had not a wink of sleep in consequence.

"Well," said my father, "that comes of not liking cats. You should get a pussycat to take care of you."

She grumbled something and retired. She later moved her quarters to the nursery, but there it was yet easier for me to plague her. I passed the string with the rat at the end of it over the middle of a bar that ran across just above her head, then took the string through a little hole in the door. As soon as I judged her safe in bed, I dropped the rat with a plump on or very near her face. I heard her give a loud cry, but before she could reach the door, I had fastened the string to a nail and got out of the way.

Mrs. Mitchell had to go to the kitchen for a light, where the fire never went out summer or winter. Afraid lest on her return she should search the bed, find my harmless animal suspended by the neck, and descend upon me with wrath, I crept into the room, retrieved my rat and string, and escaped. The next morning she went to a neighbor's and brought home a fine cat. I laughed, thinking how little her cat could protect her from my rat.

Once more, however, the Kelpie changed her quarters, to a spare room in the upper part of the house—which suited me still better. From my own bed I could now manage to drop and pull up the rat, drawing it away beyond the danger of discovery. That night she took the cat into the room with her, and I judged it prudent to leave her alone. But the next night, having secured Kirsty's cat, I turned him into the room after she was in bed: the result was a frightful explosion of feline wrath.

I now thought I might boast of my successes to Turkey, but he was not pleased. "She is sure to find you out, Ranald," he said, "and then whatever else we do will be a failure. Leave her alone till we have her."

I found one night that she was not in the house, and discovered also that her private meal tub was now empty. I ran to Turkey, and together we hurried to Betty's cottage.

It was a cloudy night with glimpses of moonlight. We heard voices talking within the cottage, and were satisfied that both the Kelpie and Wandering Willie were there.

"We must wait till she comes out," said Turkey. "We must be able to say we saw her."

There was a great stone standing out of the ground not far from the door, just opposite the elder tree, and the path lay between them.

"You get behind that stone, and I'll get behind the tree," said Turkey. "When the Kelpie comes out, you make a noise like a beast, and rush at her on all-fours."

"I'm good at a pig, Turkey," I said. "Will a pig do?"

"Yes, well enough."

"But what if she should know me, and catch me?"

"She will start away from you to my side, and I shall rush out like a mad dog, and then she'll run for it."

We waited a long time—a very long time, it seemed to me. I was just falling asleep, but the sound of the latch lifting brought me wide awake at once. I peeped from behind my shelter. It was the Kelpie, with an empty bag in her hand. Behind her came Wandering Willie, but he did not follow her from the door. The moment was favorable, for the moon was under a thick cloud. Just as she reached the stone, I rushed out on my hands and knees, grunting and squeaking like a very wild pig. Mrs. Mitchell darted aside, and I retreated behind my stone.

Then Turkey rushed at her with imitated canine fury, and from all the fierce growls and barks and squeals you would have thought he was ready to tear a whole army to pieces. She took to her heels at once. But I had hardly concealed myself behind the stone, repressing my laughter, when I was seized from behind and pommelled by Wandering Willie, who had no fear either of pig or dog.

"Turkey! Turkey!" I cried.

The cry stopped Turkey's barking pursuit of the Kelpie, and he rushed to my aid. But when he saw Willie, he turned at once for the cottage, crying, "Now for a kick at the bagpipes!"

Willie was not too much of a fool to remember and understand. He left me, and made for the cottage. Turkey drew back and let him enter, then closed the door and held it.

"Get away a bit, Ranald. I can run faster than Willie. You'll be out of sight in a few yards."

But instead of coming after us, Wandering Willie began

playing a most triumphant tune upon his darling bagpipes. We set off to outrun the Kelpie. It did not matter to Turkey, but she might lock me out again.

I was almost in bed before I heard her come in. She went straight to her own room.

CHAPTER TWENTY-EIGHT

A Double Exposure

When Mrs. Mitchell had set our porridge on the table, she stood up, and, with her fists in her sides, addressed my father.

"I'm very sorry, sir, to have to make complaints. It's a thing I don't like, and I'm not given to. I'm sure I try to do my duty by Master Ranald as well as everyone else in this house."

I felt a little confused, for I now saw clearly enough that my father could not approve of our proceedings. I whispered to Allister, "Run and fetch Turkey."

Allister set off at once. The Kelpie looked suspicious as he left the room, but she had no pretext for interference. I allowed her to tell her tale without interruption. After relating exactly what we had done the night before, when she had gone on "a visit of mercy," she accused me of all my former tricks, and ended by saying that if she were not protected against me and Turkey, she must leave the place.

"Let her go, Father," I said. "None of us like her."

"I like her," whimpered little Davie.

"Silence, sir!" said my father, very sternly. "Are these things true?"

"Yes, Father," I answered. "But please hear what *I've* got to say. She's only told you *her* side!"

"You have confessed to the truth of what she alleges," said my father. "I did think," he went on, both in sorrow and in anger, "that you had turned from your bad ways. To think of my taking you with me to the deathbed of a holy man, and then finding you playing such tricks!"

"I don't say it was right, Father, and I'm very sorry if I have offended you."

"You *have* offended me, and very deeply. You have been unkind and indeed cruel to a good woman who has done her best for you for many years!"

"I can't say I'm sorry for what I've done to her," I said.

"Really, Ranald, you are impertinent. I would send you out of the room at once, but you must beg Mrs. Mitchell's pardon first, and after that there will be something more to say, I fear."

"But, Father, you have not heard *my* story yet."

"Well—go on. It is fair to hear both sides. But nothing can justify such conduct."

With a trembling voice, I told the tale from the beginning. Before I had ended, Turkey made his appearance, ushered in by Allister. Both were out of breath with running.

My father stopped me, and ordered Turkey away until I finished. I looked up at the Kelpie once or twice. She had grown white, and grew whiter. When Turkey left the room, she would have gone too. But my father told her she must stay and hear me to the end. Several times she broke out, accusing me of telling a pack of wicked lies, but my father told her she should have an opportunity to defend herself later. When I was done, he called Turkey, and made him tell the story. Although he questioned us closely, he found no discrepancy between our accounts. He turned at last to Mrs. Mitchell, who, but for all her rage, would have been in an abject condition.

"Now, Mrs. Mitchell!" he said.

She had nothing to reply beyond stating that Turkey and I had always hated and persecuted her, and had now told a pack of lies to ruin her, a poor lone woman, with no friends to take her part.

"I do not think it likely they could be so wicked," said my father.

"So I'm to be the only wicked person in the world! Very well, sir! I will leave the house this very day."

"No, no, Mrs. Mitchell—that won't do. One party or the other *is* very wicked—that is clear; and it is of the greatest consequence to me to find out which. If you go, I shall know it is you, and have you taken up and tried for stealing. Meantime I shall go the round of the parish. I do not think all the poor people will have combined to lie against you."

"They all hate me," said the Kelpie.

"And why?" asked my father.

She made no answer.

"I must get at the truth. You can go now," said my father.

She left the room without another word, and my father turned to Turkey.

"I am surprised at you, Turkey, lending yourself to such silly pranks. Why did you not come and tell me?"

"I am very sorry, sir. I was afraid you would be troubled at finding how wicked she was, and I thought we might frighten her away somehow. But Ranald began his tricks without letting me know, and then I saw that mine could be of no use, for she would suspect them after his. Mine would have been better, sir."

"I have no doubt of it, but equally unjustifiable. And you also acted the part of an animal last night."

"Yes, but I knew it could do no good. It was all for the pleasure of frightening her. It was very foolish of me, and I beg your pardon, sir."

"Well, Turkey, you have vexed me, not by trying to find out the wrong she was doing to me and the whole parish, but by taking the whole thing into your own hands. It is worse of you, inasmuch as you are older and far wiser than Ranald. It is worse of Ranald because I am his father. I will try to show you the wrong you have done. Had you told me without doing anything yourselves, then I might have succeeded in bringing Mrs. Mitchell to repentance. I could have reasoned with her on the matter, and shown her that she was not merely a thief of the worst kind, a Judas who robbed the poor, and so robbed God. I could have shown her how cruel she was—"

"Please, sir," interrupted Turkey, "I don't think she did it for herself. I do believe that Wandering Willie is some relation of hers. He is the only poor person, almost the only person except Davie, I ever saw her behave kindly to. He was there last night, and also, I fancy, that other time when Ranald got such a fright. She must have poor relations somewhere, and sends the meal to them by Willie. You remember, sir, there were no old clothes of Allister's to be found when you wanted them for Jamie Duff."

"You may be right, Turkey. I hope you are, for though bad enough, that would not be quite so bad as doing it for herself."

"I am very sorry, Father," I said. "I beg your pardon."

"I hope it will be a lesson to you, my boy. After that you have done, rousing every bad and angry passion in her, I fear it will be of no use to try to make her be sorry and repent. It is to her, not to me, you have done the wrong. I have nothing to complain of for myself—quite the contrary. But it is a very dreadful thing to throw difficulties in the way of repentance and turning from evil works."

"What can I do to make up for it?" I sobbed.

"I don't see at this moment what you can do. I will turn it over in my mind. You may go now."

Turkey and I walked away—I to school, he to his cattle. Turkey looked sad, and I was subdued and concerned.

Everything my father heard from the poor confirmed our tale. But before he returned to the house, the Kelpie had disappeared. Many little things were missed from the house afterward, but nothing of great value, and neither she nor Wandering Willie ever appeared again.

My father gave five shillings from his own pocket to every one of the poor people whom the Kelpie had defrauded. Her place in the house was, to our endless happiness, taken by Kirsty. She faithfully carried out my father's instructions that, along with the sacred handful of meal, a penny should be given to every one of the parish poor.

Not even little Davie cried when he found that Mrs. Mitchell was really gone. It was more his own affection than her kindness that had attached him to her.

Thus were we at last delivered from the Kelpie.

CHAPTER TWENTY-NINE

Tribulation

After the Kelpie's expulsion, and the accession of Kirsty, things went on peaceably at home, but school was a different matter.

There were two schools in the little town. The first was the parish school, whose master was appointed by the presbytery. The second school was one chiefly upheld by the dissenters of the place, and the master was appointed by the parents of the scholars. Yet I do not think the second school would ever have existed except that one school was not enough for the population. So there was little real schism in the matter, except between the boys themselves. They made far more of it than their parents, and an occasional outbreak was the consequence.

There was at the second school a very rough lad named Scroggie—the least developed beyond the brute, perhaps, of all the scholars of the village. This youth, a lad of seventeen, whether moved by dislike or the mere fascination of injury, was in the habit of teasing me beyond the verge of endurance. I did not like to complain to my father, though that would have been better than to hate the lad as I did. I was ashamed of my own impotence for self-defense, but I was not more than half his size, and certainly not half his strength. My pride forbade flight, and when we met in an out-of-the-way place, Scroggie would block my path, pull my hair, pinch my cheeks, and do everything to annoy me. If we met in a street, or other people were in sight, he would pass me with a wink and a grin, as much as to say, "Wait."

One of the short but fierce wars between the rival schools

broke out. It had not endured a day before it came to a pitched battle after school hours. The second school was small, but had the advantage of being perched on top of a low, steep hill—and ours lay at the bottom. Our battles always began with rock-throwing, yet few serious accidents occurred. We had little chance against the stone-showers which descended upon us like hail, unless we charged right up the hill in the face of the inferior but well-posted enemy.

I usually collected stones for my companions, for it seemed to me that every boy, down to the smallest in either school, was skillful in throwing them, except myself. On this occasion, however, I made my first attempt to organize a troop for an uphill charge. I was now a tall boy, and of some influence among those of my own age. Whether the enemy saw our intent and proceeded to forestall it, I cannot say, but certainly that charge never took place.

A house was then being built just on the top of the hill, and a hand wagon was used to move the large stones needed. As the battle heated up, we received first the chips from the dressing of those stones. Then our adversaries laid hold of this chariot and turned it into an engine of war. They dragged it to the top of the hill, jumped upon it, and thundered down upon our troops. Vain was the storm of stones which assailed their advance: they could not have stopped if they would. My company had to open and make way for the advancing wonder, upon which towered my personal enemy Scroggie.

"Now!" I called to my men. "As soon as the thing stops, rush in and seize them! They're not half our number, and it will be an endless disgrace to let them go."

But as soon as the chariot reached a part of the hill where the slope was less, it turned a little to one side, and Scroggie fell off, drawing half of the load after him. My men rushed in with shouts of defiance, and I sprung to seize Scroggie. He tried to get up, but fell back with a groan. The moment I saw his face, my mood changed. My hatred turned all at once into pity or something better. In a moment I was down on my knees beside him. His face was white, and drops of sweat stood upon his forehead. He lay upon his side, and with one hand he scooped handfuls of dirt from the road and threw them down again. His leg was broken.

I got him to lean his head against me, and tried to make him lie more comfortably. I sent one of our swiftest runners for the doctor, and in the meantime did the best I could for him, though he did not even thank me. When the doctor came, we laid Scroggie upon the wagon, and dragged him up the hill and home to his mother.

And that was the end of that incident—for the time being.

At the last school examination I had, at the request of one of the clergymen, read aloud a metrical composition of my own—an essay on patriotism. After this the master, Mr. Wilson, had shown me a great increase of favor. Perhaps he recognized in me some germ of literary talent: it has never come to much if he did, and he must be greatly disappointed, seeing that I labor not in living words, but in dead stones. I am certain, though, that whether I build good or bad houses, I should have built worse had I not had the insight he gave me into literature and the nature of literary expression. I think that what certain successful men want to make them real artists is simply a knowledge of the literature of the country.

My brother Tom had left the school, and gone to the county town to receive some final preparation for the University. Consequently, so far as the school was concerned, I was no longer in the position of a younger brother. Also Mr. Wilson had discovered that I had some ability to impart my knowledge, and had begun to use me in teaching the others. A good deal was done this way in the Scotch schools. The master, at any moment, would choose the one he thought fit, and set him to teach a class, while he attended to individuals or taught another class himself. Nothing can be better for the verification of knowledge, or for the discovery of ignorance, than the attempt to teach.

The increasing trust the master reposed in me, and the

increasing favor which openly accompanied it, so stimulated my natural vanity, that at length it appeared in the form of presumption, and influenced my behavior to my schoolmates. Hence, a complaint arose that I was the master's favorite.

When teaching a class, I would frequently climb into Mr. Wilson's vacant chair, and sit there as if I were the master of the school. I even went so far as to keep some of my books on the master's desk. Yet I had not the least suspicion of the indignation I was rousing against me.

One afternoon I had a class of history. They read very badly, with what seemed willful blundering—but when it came to the questioning on the lesson, I soon saw there had been a conspiracy. Their answers were invariably wrong, generally absurd, and sometimes utterly grotesque. One or two girls, infected with the spirit of the game, soon outdid the whole class in the wildness of their replies. This at last got the better of me; I lost my temper, threw down my book, and retired to my seat, leaving the class where it stood.

The master called me and asked me the reason. I told him the truth of the matter. He grew very angry, and severely punished several of the bigger boys. Whether those few supposed that I had mentioned them in particular (which I did not) I do not know—but I could read in their faces that they vowed vengeance in their hearts. When school broke up, I lingered inside in the hope they would all go home as usual. But when I came out with the master, and saw the silent waiting groups, it was evident there was more thunder in the moral atmosphere than would be easily discharged. Mr. Wilson had come to the same conclusion, for he walked with me part of the way home, without alluding to the reason. Allister was with us, and I led Davie by the hand: it was his first week of school life.

When Mr. Wilson believed me quite safe, he turned into a footpath and went through the fields back toward the town, while we, delivered from all immediate apprehension, jogged homeward.

When we had gone some distance farther, I looked back, and saw a crowd following us at full speed. Then they broke the silence with a shout, followed by the patter of their many footsteps.

"Run, Allister!" I cried. I caught up Davie on my back, and ran with the feet of fear. Allister was soon far ahead of me. "Bring Turkey!" I cried after him.

"Yes, yes, Ranald!" shouted Allister, and ran yet faster.

The crowd began to pick up stones as they ran, and we soon heard the rocks hailing on the road behind us. Soon the stones began to go bounding past us, so that I dared no longer carry Davie on my back. I had to stop, which lost us time, and shift him into my arms, which made running much harder. Davie kept calling, "Run, Ranald! Here they come!" and jumping so, half in fear, half in pleasure, that I found running very hard work indeed.

Their taunting voices reached me at length, loaded with all sorts of taunting and insulting words—some deserved, but not all. Next a stone struck me, though not in a dangerous place. The bridge was now in sight, however, and there I could get rid of Davie and turn at bay. It was a small wooden bridge, with rails and a narrow gate at the end to keep horsemen from riding over it. The foremost of our pursuers were within a few yards of my heels, when I bounded on the bridge. I had just time to set Davie down and turn and shut the gate. I had just enough breath to cry, "Run, Davie!" Davie, however, had no notion of the state of affairs, and did not run, but stood behind me staring.

If Davie had only run, I would have jumped into the deep water there. If I could have reached the mill on the opposite bank, a shout would have brought the miller to my aid. But so long as I could prevent them from opening the gate, I thought I could hold the position. There was only a latch to secure it, but I pulled a thin knife from my pocket and jammed it over the latch through the iron staple. Just then I was knocked backward by a blow in the face from the first arrival. But I was up the next moment, and kicked a few of the fingers fumbling to remove the knife. To protect the latch was now my main objective, but twenty of them would have been over the top in an instant.

Then lame Scroggie strode heavily up to the gate. Recalling nothing but his old enmity, I turned once more and implored Davie, "Do run, Davie, dear!" Turning again in despair, I saw Scroggie hoisting his lame leg over the gate. I could *not* kick that leg, so I sprang up and hit Scroggie hard in the face. I might as well have hit a block of granite. He swore at me, caught my hand, turned to the assailants, and said, "Now you be off! I'll do for him!"

Though they were reluctant to obey his orders, they were not willing to turn him into an enemy, and so hung back expectant. Meantime the lame leg was on one side of the gate—the splints of which were sharpened at the points— and the sound leg was upon the other. He let go of my hand in order to support himself, and I retreated, trembling, though my enemies on the other side could not reach me so long as Scroggie was upon the gate. The lame leg went searching gently about, but could find no rest for its foot. Scroggie's repose upon the top was anything but perfect, and the leg suspended behind was useless. The long and the short (both in legs and results) was that Scroggie was stuck—and so long as he was stuck, I was safe.

I turned and caught up Davie, heading for home once more. But that very instant there was a new rush at the gate; Scroggie was hoisted over, the knife was taken out, and on poured the assailants, before I had reached the other end of the bridge.

"At them, Oscar!" cried Turkey from ahead of me.

The dog rushed past me on to the bridge, followed by Turkey. I set Davie down and breathed again. There was a scurry and a rush, a splash or two in the water, and then back came Oscar with his innocent tongue hanging out like a blood-red banner of victory. He was followed by Scroggie, exploding with laughter.

Oscar wagged his tail, and looking as pleased as if he had

restored obedience to a flock of unruly sheep. I shrank from Scroggie, wishing Turkey, who was still at the other end of the bridge, would make haste.

"Wasn't it fun, Ranald?" Scroggie asked. "Did you think I was so lame that I couldn't get over that gate? I was stuck on purpose."

Turkey joined us with an inquiring look, for he knew how Scroggie had been in the habit of treating me.

"It's all right, Turkey," I said. "Scroggie stuck on the gate on purpose."

"A good thing for you, Ranald!" said Turkey. "Didn't you see Peter Mason among them?"

"No. He left the school last year."

"He was there, though, and I doubt he meant to be agreeable."

"I tell you what," said Scroggie. "If you like, I'll leave my school and come to yours."

I thanked him, but said I did not think there would be more of it.

Allister and I told my father as much as we knew of the affair.

The next morning, just as we were all settling to work, my father entered the school. The hush that followed was intense. The ringleaders of my enemies held down their heads, anticipating an outbreak of vengeance. But after a few moments conversation with Mr. Wilson, my father departed. There was a mystery about the proceeding which had a very sedative effect the whole of the morning.

When we broke up for dinner, Mr. Wilson detained me, and told me that my father thought it better that, for the moment, I should not hold such a prominent position as before. The master said I had been a great help to him, but if I did not object, he would ask my father to allow me to assist him in the evening school during the winter. I was delighted at the prospect, sank back into my natural position, and met with no further annoyance. After a while I was able to assure my former foes that I had had no voice in bringing punishment upon them in particular, and the enmity was quite extinguished.

When the evening school opened, Mr. Wilson called at the manse, and my father agreed to the arrangement. The scholars were mostly young men from neighboring farms or from workshops in the village. Though I was younger than they, there was no danger of jealousy.

There were a few girls at the school as well, among them Elsie Duff. Elsie was now able to have a little more of her own way, and there was no real reason why Elsie's grandmother should not be left for an hour or two in the evening. I need hardly say that Turkey was a regular attendant. He always, and I often, saw Elsie home.

My chief pleasure lay in helping Elsie with her lessons. I did my best to assist all who wanted my aid, but offered unsolicited attention to her. She was not quick, but would never be satisfied until she understood. Turkey was far before me in trigonometry, but I was able to help him in grammar and geography and Latin.

Sometimes Mr. Wilson would ask me to go home with him after school and take supper. He had an excellent little library, and would take down his favorite books and read me passages. It is wonderful how things which, in reading for ourselves, we might pass over in a half-blind manner, gain their true power and influence through the voice of one who sees and feels what is in them. If a man in whom you have confidence merely lays his finger on a paragraph and says to you, "Read that," you will probably discover three times as much in it as you would if you had only chanced upon it in the course of your reading. In such case the mind gathers itself up, and is all eyes and ears.

But Mr. Wilson would sometimes read me a few verses of his own—a delight I have rarely experienced. I wondered that a full-grown man and good scholar should treat me as an equal, but sympathy is precious even from a child, and Mr. Wilson had no companions of his own standing. I believe he read more to Turkey than to me, however.

CHAPTER THIRTY

A Winter's Ride

In this same winter there came a tremendous fall of snow. A furious wind, lasting two days and the night between, drifted the snow into great mounds, so that the shape of the country was much altered with new heights and hollows. Even those who were best acquainted with the roads could only guess at their direction, and it was easy to lose the right track, even in broad daylight. As soon as the storm was over, folk had begun to cut passages through some of the deeper wreaths, as they called the snow mounds. And over the tops of others, and along the general line of the roads, footpaths were soon trodden. But it was many days before wagons or coaches could pass.

All the short day, the low sun was brilliant, and the whole country shone with dazzling whiteness—but after the sun set at four o'clock, nothing more dreary can be imagined. Keen winds rushed in gusts from the northeast, lifted the snow-powder from untrodden shadows, and blew it stinging in the face of the freezing traveler.

About three o'clock one afternoon, just as I came home from school, my father received a message by a groom on horseback that a certain laird, whose house lay three or four miles off among the hills, was at the point of death, and very anxious to see him. My father at once made ready for the uninviting journey.

Since my brother Tom's departure, I had become yet more of a companion to my father, and now I begged to be allowed to go with him. His little black mare had given birth to a foal—a daughter—almost twice her mother's size, and a bit clumsy. Still she had a touch of the roadster in her, and could get over the ground well enough with a sort of speedy slouch. She was strong, and could go through the wreaths, Andrew said, like a red-hot iron.

My father looked out at the sky, and hesitated. "I hardly know what to say, Ranald. If I were sure of the weather—but I am very doubtful. However, if it should break up, we can stay there all night. Yes. Here, Allister—run and tell Andrew to saddle both the mares, and bring them down directly. Make haste with your dinner, Ranald."

Delighted at the prospect, I made haste. In half an hour we were all mounted and on our way. The groom, who had so lately traversed the road, rode a few yards in front.

Our horses made very slow progress. It was almost nowhere possible to trot, and we had to plod on, step by step. This made it easier to talk.

As we grew older, we had drawn nearer to my father—or, more properly, my father had drawn us nearer to him, dropping, by degrees, that reticence which, perhaps too many parents keep up until their children are full grown. As much as he hated certain kinds of gossip, he believed that indifference to your neighbor and his affairs was worse. He said everything depended on the spirit in which men spoke of each other; that much of what was called gossip was only a natural love of biography, and, if kindly, was better than blameless. He called the greater part of it objectionable, simply because it was not loving, only curious. And another portion was among the wickedest things on earth, because it had for its object both to believe and to make others believe the worst.

"The country looks dreary, doesn't it, Ranald?" my father said.

"Just as if everything were dead, Father," I replied.

"If the sun were to cease shining altogether, what do you think would happen?"

I thought a bit, but had no answer.

"What makes the seed grow, Ranald," he continued, "the

oats, and the wheat, and the barley?"

"The rain, Father."

"Well, if there were no sun, the vapors would not rise to make clouds. What rain there was already in the sky would come down in snow or lumps of ice. The earth would grow colder and harder, until at last it went sweeping through the air, one frozen mass, as hard as a stone, without a green leaf or a living creature left."

"How dreadful, Father!"

"Yes, my boy. The sun is the life of the world. Not only does he make the rain rise to fall on the seeds in the earth, but even that would be useless if he did not make them warm as well—and do something else besides which we cannot understand. Further down into the earth than any of the rays of light can reach, he sends other rays we cannot see, which go searching about like long fingers—and wherever they find and touch a seed, the life in that seed begins to talk to itself, and straightway begins to grow. Out of the dark earth the sun thus brings all the lovely green things of the spring, and clothes the world with beauty, and sets the waters running, and the birds singing, and the lambs bleating, and the children gathering daisies and buttercups, and the gladness overflowing in all hearts. Very different from what we see now, isn't it, Ranald?"

"Yes, Father. A body can hardly believe, to look at it now, that the world will ever be like that again."

"But as cold and wretched as it looks, the sun has not forsaken it. He has only drawn away from it a little, for good reasons, one of which is that we may learn that we cannot do without him. If he were to go, not one breath more could one of us draw. Horses and men, we should drop down frozen lumps, as hard as stones. Who is the sun's father, Ranald?"

"He hasn't got a father," I replied, hoping for an answer to the riddle.

"Yes, he has, Ranald: I can prove that. You remember whom the Apostle James calls the Father of Lights?"

"Oh yes, of course, Father. But doesn't that mean another kind of lights?"

"Yes. But they couldn't be called lights if they were not like the sun. All kinds of lights must come from the Father of Lights. Now the Father of the sun must be like the sun and, indeed of all material things, the sun is the most like God. We pray to God to shine upon us and give us light. If God did not shine into our hearts, they would be dead lumps of cold."

"Then, Father, God never stops shining upon us. He wouldn't be like the sun if He did. For even in winter the sun shines enough to keep us alive."

"True, my boy. I am very glad you understand me. I have never yet known a man in whose heart I could not find proofs of the shining of the great Sun. It might be a very feeble wintry shine, but still He was there. For a human heart though, it is very dreadful to have a cold, white winter like this inside it instead of a summer of color and warmth and light. There's the poor old man we are going to see. They talk of the winter of age: that's all very well, but the heart is not made for winter. A man may have the snow on his roof, and merry children about his heart; he may have gray hairs on his head, and the very gladness of summer in his bosom. But this old man, I am afraid, feels wintry cold inside."

"Then why doesn't the Father of Lights shine more on him and make him warmer?"

"The sun is shining as much on the earth in the winter as in the summer: why is the earth no warmer?"

"Because it is turned away from the sun."

"Just so. Then if a man turns himself away from the Father of Lights—the great Sun—how can he be warmed?"

"But the earth can't help it, Father."

"But the man can, Ranald. He feels the cold, and he knows he can turn to the Light. Even this poor old man knows it now. God is shining on him—a wintry way—or he would not feel the cold at all; he would only be a lump of ice, a part of the very winter itself. The good of what warmth God gives him is that he feels cold. If he were all cold, he couldn't feel cold."

"Does he want to turn to the Sun, then?"

"I do not know. I only know that he is miserable because he has not turned to the Sun."

"What will you say to him, Father?"

"It depends on what I find him thinking. Of all things, my boy, keep your face to the Sun. You can't shine of yourself, you can't be good of yourself, but God has made you able to turn to the Sun whence all goodness and all shining comes. God's children may be very naughty, but they must be able to turn toward Him. The Father of Lights is the Father of every weakest little baby of a good thought in us, as well as of the highest devotion of martyrdom. If you turn your face to the Sun, my boy, your soul will, when you come to die, feel like an autumn, with golden fruits of the earth hanging in rich clusters ready to be gathered—not like a winter. You may feel ever so worn, but you will not feel withered. You will die in peace, hoping for the spring—and such a spring!"

Thus talking, in the course of two hours we arrived at the dwelling of the old laird.

CHAPTER THIRTY-ONE
The Peat Stack

How dreary the old house looked as we approached it
through the gathering darkness! All the light appeared to
come from the snow which rested wherever it could lie—on
roofs and window ledges and turrets. Not a glimmer shone
from the windows.

"Surely nobody lives *there,* Father," I said.

"It does not look very lively," he answered.

The house stood on a bare knoll. There was not a tree
within sight, and rugged hills arose on all sides of it. There
was a brook, but it lay frozen beneath yards of snow. For
miles in any direction those gusts might wander without
shaking door or window, or carrying with them a puff of
smoke from any hearth. We crossed the yard at the back of
the house, then dismounted on a few feet of rough pavement
which had been swept clear. An old woman came to the
door, and led us into a dreary parlor without even a fire to
welcome us.

After some time, the housekeeper returned, and invited
my father to go to the laird's room. As they went, he
requested her to take me to the kitchen next, which she did.
The fire, though very small, was most welcome. She laid a
few more peats upon it, and encouraged them to a blaze,
remarking, with a sidelong look, "We daren't do this, you
see, sir, if the laird was about. The honest man would call it
waste."

"Is he dying?" I asked, for the sake of saying something.
She only shook her head for reply, went to a press at the
other end of the large vault-like kitchen, brought me some

milk in a basin and some oatcake upon a platter and said, "It's not my house, or I would set something better before the minister's son."

I was glad of any food, however, and it was well for me that I ate heartily. I was quite warm before my father stepped into the kitchen, very solemn. He neither sat down nor accepted the refreshment the old woman offered him.

"We must be going," he objected, "for it looks stormy, and the sooner we set out the better."

"I'm sorry I can't ask you to stop the night," she said, "for I couldn't make you comfortable. There's nothing fit to offer you in the house, and there's not a bed that's been slept in for I don't know how long."

"Never mind," said my father cheerfully. "The moon is up already, and I trust we shall get home before the snow begins to fall. Will you have the man get the horses out?"

When she returned from her errand, she asked my father in a loud whisper, "Is he in a bad way, sir?"

"He is dying," answered my father.

"I know that," she returned. "He'll be gone before the morning. But is he in a bad way for the other world?"

"Well, my good woman, after a life like his, we are only too glad to remember what our Lord told us—not to judge. I do think he is ashamed and sorry for his past life. But it's not the wrong he has done in former time that stands in his way, but his present fondness for what he counts his own. It breaks his heart to leave all his little bits of property— particularly the money he has saved—and yet he has some hope that Jesus Christ will be kind enough to pardon him. He will find himself very miserable though, when he has not one scrap left to call his own."

"It's dreadful to think of him flying through the air on a night like this," she said.

"My good woman," returned my father, "we know nothing about where or how the departed spirit exists after it has left the body. But it seems to me just as dreadful to be without God in the world as to be without Him anywhere else. Let us pray for him that God may be with him wherever he is."

We knelt, and my father prayed earnestly to God for the old man. Then we rose, mounted our horses, and rode away.

We were only halfway home when the clouds began to cover the moon and the snow began to fall. Hitherto we had gotten on pretty well, for there was light enough to see the feeble track. Now, however, we had to keep a careful lookout. We pressed our horses, and they went bravely, but it was slow work at the best. It grew darker and darker, for the clouds went on gathering, and the snow was coming down in huge dull flakes. Faster and thicker they came, until we could not see the road before us, and were compelled to leave all to the wisdom of our horses. My father, having great confidence in his own little mare, rode first. I followed close behind.

Father kept talking to me very cheerfully to prevent me from getting frightened. But I had not a thought of fear, for to be with my father was to me perfect safety. He was telling me how, on more occasions than one, Missy had gotten him through places where the road was impassable by walking on the tops of the walls, when all at once both our horses plunged into a gulf of snow. The more my mare struggled, the deeper we sank, and I thought it was closing over my head.

"Father! Father!" I shouted.

"Don't be frightened, my boy!" cried my father. His voice seemed to come from far away. "We are in God's hands. I can't help you now, but as soon as Missy is quiet I shall come to you. I think I know where we are. We've dropped right off the road. You're not hurt, are you?"

"No," I answered. "I was only frightened."

My mare soon lay, or rather stuck quiet, with her neck and head thrown back and her body deep in the snow. I put up my hands to feel, but the snow rose above my head farther than I could reach. I wriggled clear of the stirrups and scrambled up, first on my knees, and then on my feet. Standing on the saddle, I stretched my hands above my head, but still the broken wall of snow ascended. I could see nothing of my father, but I heard him talking to Missy.

My fear was now quite gone, and I felt like laughing at the fun of the misadventure. I had as yet no idea of how serious a thing it might be. Still I had sense enough to see that something must be done—but what? I saw no way of getting out of the hole except by trampling down the snow upon the back of my poor mare, and that I could not think of. And I doubted that even my father could tell where to turn for help or shelter. Finding our way home, even if we got free, seemed out of the question.

My mare began plunging violently, and I found myself thrown against some hard substance. I thrust my hand through the snow, and felt what I thought might be the stones of a wall. I might clear away enough of the snow to climb upon that—but then what next?

"Ranald!" cried my father. "How do you get on?"

"Much the same, Father," I answered.

"I'm out of the wreath," he returned. "We've come through the other side. You are better where you are, however. The snow is warmer than the air, and it is beginning to blow. Pull your feet out and get right upon the mare's back."

"That's just where I am, Father—lying on her back, and pretty comfortable," I rejoined.

All this time the snow was falling thickly. If it went on like this, I would be buried before morning, and the rising wind added to the danger of it. We were at the wrong end of the night too.

"I'm in a kind of ditch, I think, Father," I cried, "between the place we fell off on one side and a stone wall on the other."

"That can hardly be or I shouldn't have got out," he returned. "But now I've got Missy quiet, I'll come to you. I must get you out, I see, or you will be snowed up."

The next moment he gave a joyous exclamation.

"What is it, Father?"

"It's not a stone wall—it's a peat stack!"

"I don't see what good it is. We can't light a fire."

"No, my boy, but where there's a peat stack, there's probably a house." He began shouting at the top of his voice and listening for a response. This lasted a good while, and I began to get very cold.

"I'm nearly frozen, Father," I said, "and what's to become of my poor mare? She's got no clothes on!"

"I'll get you out, my boy, and then at least you will be able to move about a little." I heard him shovelling at the snow with his hands and feet. "I've got one of the mare's ears," he said next. "I won't try to get her out until I get you off her."

I put out my hand and felt along my mare's neck. What a joy it was to catch my father's hand through the darkness and the snow! He grasped mine and drew me toward him, then clasped me by the arm and began dragging me through the snow. The mare began plunging again, and by her struggles assisted my father. In a few moments he had me in his arms.

"Thank God!" he said, as he set me down against the peat stack. "Stand there—she must fight her way out now." He went back to the mare, and went on clearing away the snow. Then I could hear him patting and encouraging her. Next I heard a great blowing and scrambling, and at last a snort and the thunder of hooves.

"Whoa! Gently! She's off!" cried my father.

My mare's mother gave one snort, and away they both thundered. Their sounds were soon quenched in the snow.

"There's a business!" said my father. "I'm afraid the poor things will only go farther to fare worse. We are as well without them, however, and if they should find their way home, so much the better for us. They might have kept us a little warmer though. We must fight the cold as best we can for the rest of the night, for it would be folly to leave here before it is light."

Suddenly I remembered how I had burrowed in the straw to hide myself after running from Dame Shand's. With a little loosening I succeeded in drawing out a peat.

"Father," I said, "couldn't we make a hole in the peat stack and build ourselves in?"

"A capital idea, my boy!" he answered, with a gladness in his voice at finding that I had some practical sense in me. "We'll try it at once."

"I've got two or three out already," I said. It was easy enough after one had been started.

"We must take care we don't bring down the whole stack though," said my father.

"Even then," I returned, "we could build ourselves up in them, and that would be something."

"Right, Ranald. It would be only making houses to our own shape instead of big enough to move about in—turning crustaceous animals, you know."

"It would be a peat greatcoat at least," I remarked, pulling away.

"Here," he said, "I will put my stick under the top row. That will be a lintel to support above."

We worked with a will, piling up the peats a little in front that we might with them build up the door of our cave after we were inside. We grew quite merry over it.

"We shall be brought before the magistrates for destruction of property," said my father.

"You'll have to send Andrew to build up the stack again—that's all."

Every now and then a few peats would come down with a rush, and before long we had made a large hole. We left a good thick floor to sit upon.

Creeping in, we commenced building up the entrance. We had not proceeded far, however, before we found that our cave was too small, and that as we should have to remain in it for hours, we must find it very cramped. Therefore, instead of using any more of the peats already pulled out, we finished building up the wall with others fresh drawn from the inside. When we had finished, we sat down to wait for the morning. My father was as calm as if he had been seated in his study chair, and I was in a state of condensed delight—for was not this a grand adventure, with my father to share it, and keep it from going too far?

He sat with his head back leaning against the side of the hole, and I sat between his knees, and leaned against him. His arms were folded round me, and could ever a boy be more blessed than I was then? Mine was both the sense of outside danger, and the assurance of present safety and good hope. Ever since when any trouble has threatened me, I have turned to the memory of that harbor of refuge from the storm. There I sat for long hours secure in my father's arms, knowing that the soundless snow was falling thick around us. I marked occasionally the threatening wail of the wind like the cry of a wild beast scenting us from afar.

"This is grand, Father," I said.

"You would be better to be at home in bed, wouldn't you?" he asked, trying me.

"No, indeed, I should not," I answered, with more than honesty. I felt exuberantly happy.

"We must keep warm," he said. "If you should get very cold indeed, you must not lose heart, my man, but think how pleasant it will be when we get home to a good fire and a hot breakfast."

"I think I can bear it all right. I have often been cold enough at school."

"This may be worse. But we need not anticipate evil: that is to send out for the suffering. It is well to be prepared for it, but it is ill to brood over a fancied future of evil. In all my life, my boy, I have never found any trial to go beyond what I could bear. In the worst cases of suffering, I think there is help given which those who look on cannot understand, but which enables the sufferer to endure. The last help of that kind is death, which I think is always a blessing, though few people can regard it as such.

"This nest brings to my mind what the psalmist says about dwelling in the secret place of the Most High. Everyone who will may there, like the swallow, make himself a nest."

"This can't be very like that though, surely, Father," I ventured to object. "It's not safe enough."

"You are right there. Still it *is* our refuge."

"The cold does get through it, Father."

"But it keeps our minds at peace. Even the refuge in God does not always secure us from external suffering. The heart may be quite happy and strong when the hands are benumbed with cold. Yes, the heart even may grow cold with coming death while the man himself retreats the farther into the secret place of the Most High, growing more calm and hopeful as the last cold invades the house of his body. I believe that all troubles come to drive us into that refuge—that secret place where alone we can be safe. You will, when you go out into the world, my boy, find that most men not only do not believe this, but do not believe that you believe it. They regard it at best as a fantastic weakness, fit only for sickly people. But watch how the strength of such people, their calmness and common sense, fares when the grasp of suffering lays hold upon them.

"It was a sad and miserable sight I saw this afternoon. If the laird's mind had been an indication of reality, one must have said that there was no God—no God at least that would have anything to do with him. The universe as reflected in the tarnished mirror of his soul, was a chill misty void, through which blew the moaning wind of an unknown fate. As near as ever I saw it, that man was without God and without hope in the world.

"All the men who have done the mightiest things—I do not mean the showiest things—all that are like William of Orange, or John Milton, or William Penn, or any other of the cloud of witnesses spoken of in the Epistle to the Hebrews—have not only believed that there was this refuge in God, but have themselves more or less entered into the secret place of the Most High. There only could they have found strength to do their mighty deeds. They were able to do them because they knew God wanted them to do them, that He was on their side—or rather they were on His side, and therefore safe, surrounded by God on every side. My boy, do the will of God—that is, what you know or believe to be right, and fear nothing."

I never forgot the lesson. My father was not at all favorable to much talk about religion. He said that much talk prevented much thought, and talk without thought was bad. He was silent after this utterance, and full of inward repose, I fell asleep in his arms.

When I awoke I found myself very cold. My father was asleep, and for the first time I became uneasy. It was not because of the cold, for that was endurable. But the night lay awful in white silence about me, the wind was moaning outside and blowing long thin currents through the peat walls around me, and our warm home lay far away—in the midst of all these, I was awake and my father slept. I could easily have awakened him, but I was not selfish enough for that. I sat still and shivered and felt very dreary.

Then the last words of my father returned to me, and with a throb of relief, the thought awoke in my mind that although my father was asleep, the great Father of us both, He in whose heart lay that secret place of refuge, neither slumbered nor slept. And now I was able to wait in patience with a new idea, if not a sense, of the present care of God.

Finally my father stirred, and closed his arms about me again.

"I'm so glad you're awake, Father," I said.

"Have *you* been long awake then?"

"Not so very long, but I felt lonely without you."

"Are you very cold? *I* feel rather chilly."

So we chatted away for a while.

"I wonder if it is nearly day yet. I do not in the least know how long we have slept. I forgot to wind my watch last night, so if it has stopped I shall know it is near daylight."

He held his watch to his ear: alas! It was ticking vigorously. He felt for the keyhole and wound it up. After that we repeated as many of the metrical psalms and paraphrases of Scripture as we could recollect. Still the weary time went very slowly, and I was growing so cold that I could hardly bear it.

"You feel very cold to me, Ranald," said my father, folding me closer in his arms. "You must try not to go to sleep again, for that would be dangerous now. I feel more cramped than cold."

As he said this, he extended his legs and threw his head back to stretch out his uneasiness. Down came a shower of peats upon our heads and bodies, and when I tried to move, I found myself fixed. I could not help laughing.

"Father, I cried, as soon as I could speak, "you're like Samson: you've brought down the house upon us."

"So I have, my boy. It was very thoughtless of me."

"Can you move, Father? *I* can't," I said.

"I can move my legs, but I'm afraid to move even a toe in my boot for fear of bringing down another avalanche of peats. But no, there's not much danger of that: they are all down already, for I feel snow on my face."

My father struggled, but could not do much, for I lay against him under a great heap. His struggles made an opening sideways, however.

"Father! Shout!" I cried. "I see a light!"

We shouted as loud as we could, and then lay listening. My heart beat so that I was afraid I should not hear any reply that might come, but the next moment one rang through the frosty air.

"It's Turkey!" I cried. "I know his shout! Turkey! Turkey!" I shrieked, almost weeping with delight.

Again Turkey's cry rang through the darkness, and the wavering light drew nearer.

"Mind how you step, Turkey," cried my father. "There's a hole you may tumble into."

"It wouldn't hurt him much in the snow," I said.

"Perhaps not, but he would probably lose his light."

"Shout again!" cried Turkey. "I can't make out where you are."

"We're just off the road, in a peat stack."

"Oh! I know the peat stack. I'll be with you in a moment."

Turkey did not, however, find it so easily as he had expected, as the peats were covered with snow. My father gave up trying to free himself and took to laughing instead at the ridiculous situation in which we were about to be discovered. He kept directing Turkey who, after some disappearances which made us very anxious about the lantern, caught sight of the stack and walked straight toward it. Now first we saw that he was accompanied by Andrew.

"Where are you, sir?" asked Turkey, throwing the light of the lantern over the ruin.

"Buried in the peats," answered my father, laughing. "Come and get us out."

Turkey strode up to the heap, and turned the light into it. "I didn't know it had been raining peats, sir."

"The peats didn't fall quite so far as the snow, Turkey, or they would have made a worse job of it," answered my father.

Meanwhile Andrew and Turkey were both busy, and in a few moments we stood upon our feet, stiff with cold and cramped with confinement, but merry enough at heart.

"What brought you out to look for us?" asked my father.

"I heard Missy whinnying at the stable door," said Andrew. "When I saw she was alone, I knew something had happened, so I woke Turkey. We only stopped to run into the manse for a drop of whiskey to bring with us, and set out at once."

"What time is it now?" asked my father.

"About one o'clock," answered Andrew.

One o'clock! I thought. *What a time we should have had to wait!*

"Have you been long in finding us?"

"Only about an hour."

"Then the little mare must have had great trouble in getting home. You say the other was not with her?"

"No, sir. She's not made her appearance."

"Then if we don't find her she will be dead before morning. Are you able to walk, Ranald?"

"I shall be, after my legs come to themselves."

Turkey produced a bottle of milk for me, and Andrew produced the little flask of whiskey which Kirsty had sent. My father took a little of the latter while I emptied my bottle, and then we set out to look for the young mare.

"Where are we?" asked my father. "How is it that nobody heard our shouting?"

"The old man who lives nearby is as deaf as a post," answered Turkey, "and I dare say his people were all asleep."

The snow was falling only in a few large flakes now. The moon had come out again, and the white world lay around us in lovely light. A good deal of snow had fallen while we lay in the peats, but we could still trace the track of the two horses. We followed it a long way, and came to places where they had been floundering together in a wreath. At last we reached the spot where one had parted from the other. We traced one of the tracks to the road, concluded it was Missy's, and so returned to the other.

We soon came upon the poor mare lying upon her back in a deep runnel,* in which the snow was very soft. She had put her forefeet in it as she galloped heedlessly along, tumbled right over it, and now lay helpless. Turkey and Andrew had had the foresight to bring spades and a rope with them, and they set to work at once. My father took a turn now and then, and I held the lantern. It took more than an hour to get the poor thing on her legs again, but when she was up, it was all they could do to hold her. She was so wild with cold, and with delight at feeling her legs under her once more, that she would have broken loose again and galloped off.

They set me on her back, and with my father on one side, Turkey on the other, and Andrew at her head, I rode home in great comfort. It was another good hour before we arrived, and we were right glad to see through the curtains of the parlor the glow of the great fire which Kirsty had kept up for us.

CHAPTER THIRTY-TWO

The Prince and the Sea Maiden

During that winter I attended the evening school and assisted the master. I confess, however, it was not so much for the master as to be near Elsie Duff, of whom I now thought many times an hour. Her sweet face grew more and more dear to me. I suppose my condition was what people would call being in love with her, but I never thought of that: I only thought of her. Nor did I ever dream of saying a word to her on the subject. I wished nothing other than as it was. To think about her all day, to see her at night, and get near her now and then, to hear her voice and look into her tender eyes was all that I desired. It never occurred to me that things could not go on so, and that a change must come.

When school was over, I walked home with her—not alone, for Turkey was always on the other side. I had no suspicion that Turkey's admiration of Elsie could ever come into collision with mine. We joined in praising her, but my admiration ever found more words than Turkey's, and I thought my love for her was greater than his.

We seldom went into her grandmother's cottage, for she did not make us welcome. After we had taken Elsie home we generally visited Turkey's mother, where we were sure of a kind reception. She was a patient, diligent woman, who looked as if she had nearly done with life, and had only to gather up the crumbs of it. I have often wondered whether she was content to be unhappy, or whether she lived in hope of some blessedness beyond. It is marvelous with how little happiness some people can get through the world.

Surely they are inwardly sustained with something even better than joy.

"Did you ever hear my mother sing?" asked Turkey, as we sat together over her little fire on one of these occasions. The room was lighted only by a little oil lamp, for there was no flame to the fire of peats and dried oakbark.

"No, but I should like to," I answered.

"She sings such strange ballads, like you never heard," said Turkey. "Give us one, Mother, do."

She yielded, and in a low chanting voice, sang a ballad of a prince and a sea maiden.

Up came the waves of the tide with a whush,
And back went the pebbles with a whirr,
When the king's one son came walking in the hush,
To hear the sea murmur and murr.

The half moon was rising the waves abune,
And a glimmer of cold wet light
Came over the water straight from the mune,
Like a path across the night.

What's that, and that, far out in the grey
Atwixt the moon and the land?
It's the bonny sea maidens at their play—
Hold away, king's son, from the strand.

One rock stood up with a shadow at its foot:
The king's son stepped behind.
The merry sea maidens came gamboling out,
Combing their hair in the wind.

O merry their laugh when they felt the land
Under their light cool feet!
Each laid her comb on the yellow sand,
And the gladsome dance grew fleet.

But the fairest she laid her comb by itself
On the rock where the king's son lay.
He stole about, and the carven shell
He hid in his bosom away.

And he watched the dance till the clouds did gloom,
And the wind blew an angry tune:
One after one she caught up her comb,
To the sea went dancing down.

But the fairest, with hair like the moon in a cloud,
She sought till she was the last.
He creeping went and watching stood,
And he thought to hold her fast.

She dropped at his feet without motion or heed;
He took her, and home he sped.
All day she lay like a withered seaweed,
On a purple and golden bed.

But at night when the wind from the watery bars
Blew into the dusky room,
She opened her eyes like two setting stars,
And back came her twilight bloom.

The king's son knelt beside her bed:
She was his ere a month had passed.
And the cold sea maiden he had wed
Grew a tender wife at last.

And all went well till her baby was born,
And then she could not sleep;
She would rise and wander till the breaking morn,
Hark-harking the sound of the deep.

One night when the wind was wailing about,
And the sea was speckled with foam,

From room to room she went in and out
And she came on her carven comb.

She twisted her hair with eager hands,
She put in the comb with glee:
She's out and she's over the glittering sands,
And away to the moaning sea.

One cry came back from far away:
He awoke, and was all alone.
Her night robe lay on the marble gray,
And the cold sea maiden was gone.

Ever and aye from first peep of the moon,
When the wind blew off of the sea,
The desert shore still up and down
Heavy at heart paced he.

But never more came the maidens to play
From the merry cold-hearted sea;
He heard their laughter far out and away,
But heavy at heart paced he.

"That's what comes of taking what you have no right to,"
said Turkey, in whom the practical had ever the upper hand
of the imaginative.

As we walked home together later, I resumed the subject.
"I think you're too hard on the king's son," I said. "He
couldn't help falling in love with the mermaid."

"He had no business to steal her comb, and then run away
with her."

"She was none the worse for it."

"I don't think the girl herself would have said so," he
retorted. "Not every girl would care to marry a king's son.
She might have had a lover of her own down in the sea. At
all events, the prince was none the better for it."

"But she made a tender wife," I objected.

"She made the best of it. I dare say he wasn't a bad sort of fellow, but he was no gentleman."

"Turkey! He was a prince!"

"I know that."

"Then he *must* have been a gentleman."

"I don't know that. I've read of a good many princes who did things I should be ashamed to do."

"But you're not a prince, Turkey."

"No. Therefore if I were to do what was rude and dishonest, people would say, 'What could you expect of a plowboy?' A prince ought to be just so much better bred than a plowboy. I would scorn to do what that prince did. What's wrong in a plowboy can't be right in a prince, Ranald, or else right is only right sometimes—so that right may be wrong and wrong may be right, which is as much to say there is no right and wrong. And if there's no right and wrong, the world's an awful mess, and there can't be any God, for a God would never have made it like that."

"Well, Turkey, you know best. I can't help thinking the prince was not so much to blame, though."

"You see what came of it—misery."

"Perhaps he would rather have had the misery and all together than none of it."

"That's for him to settle. But he must have seen he was wrong, before he had done wandering by the sea."

"Well now, Turkey, what would you have done yourself, supposing the most beautiful of them all laid her comb down within an inch of you, and never saw you?"

Turkey thought for a moment. "Well, I'm sure I should not have kept the comb, even if I had taken it just to get a chance of speaking to her. And I can't help fancying if he had behaved like a gentleman and let her go, she might have come again. And if she had married him at last of her own free will, she would not have run away from him, let the sea call her ever so much."

The next evening I looked for Elsie as usual, but she did not come. I could see that Turkey was anxious too. The moment school was over, we two hurried away to the cottage. There we found Elsie weeping: her grandmother had died suddenly. She clung to Turkey, and seemed almost to forget my presence. But I thought nothing of that. Had the case been mine, I too should have clung to Turkey from faith in his help and superior wisdom.

There were two or three old women in the place. Turkey went and spoke to them, and then took Elsie home to his mother, where both Elsie and Jamie lived for the rest of the winter. The cottage was let, and the cow taken home by their father. Before summer, Jamie took a place in a shop in the village, and then Elsie went back to her mother.

CHAPTER THIRTY-THREE

An Evening Visit

I now saw much less of Elsie at the school, but I went with Turkey as often as I could to visit her at her father's cottage. The evenings we spent there are among the happiest hours in my memory. One evening in particular—which must have been almost the last—stands out as a type of the whole.

Turkey and I set out as the sun was going down on an evening in the end of April, when the nightly frosts had not yet vanished. The hail was dancing about us as we started, and the sun was disappearing in a bank of tawny orange cloud. The night would be cold and dark and stormy—but we cared nothing for that, as a conflict with the elements always added to the pleasure of any undertaking then. In the midst of another shower of hail, driven on the blasts of a keen wind, we arrived at the cottage. It had been built by Duff himself to receive his bride, and although since enlarged, was still a very little house. It had a foundation of stone, but the walls were of turf. He had lined it with boards, however, and so made it warm and comfortable.

When we entered, a glowing fire of peat was on the hearth, and the supper pot hung over it. Mrs. Duff was spinning, and Elsie, by the light of a little oil lamp suspended against the wall, was teaching her youngest brother to read. Mrs. Duff did not rise from her spinning, but spoke a kindly welcome. Elsie got up and set chairs for us by the fire, then took the little fellow away to bed.

"It's a cold night," said Mrs. Duff. "The wind seems to blow through me as I sit at my wheel. I wish my husband would come home."

"He'll be suppering his horses, said Turkey. "I'll just run across and give him a hand, and that'll bring him in the sooner."

"Thank you, Turkey," said Mrs. Duff as he vanished. "He's a fine lad," she remarked, much in the same phrase my father used when speaking of him.

"There's nobody like Turkey," I said.

"Indeed, I think you're right there, Ranald. A better-behaved lad doesn't step. He'll do something to distinguish himself someday. I shouldn't wonder if he went to college and wagged his head in a pulpit yet."

The idea of Turkey wagging his head in a pulpit made me laugh.

"Wait till you see," resumed Mrs. Duff, somewhat offended at my reception of her prophecy. "Folk will hear of him yet."

"I didn't mean he couldn't be a minister, Mrs. Duff. But I don't think he will take to that."

Elsie came back, lifted the lid of the pot, and examined the state of its contents. I got hold of her hand, but for the first time she withdrew it—though very gently. By the time she had put the plates and spoons upon the white deal table in the middle of the floor, the water in the pot was boiling. She began to make the porridge, at which she was judged to be first-rate—equal, in my mind, to Kirsty. By the time it was ready, her father and Turkey came in. James Duff said grace, and we sat down to our supper. The wind was blowing hard outside, and every now and then the hail came in deafening rattles against the little windows, descended the wide chimney, and danced on the floor about the hearth.

After supper, James turned to me and said, "Haven't you a song or a ballad to give us, Ranald? I know you're always getting hold of such things."

Every time I went, I tried to have something to repeat to them. As I could not sing, this was the nearest way in which I might contribute to the evening's entertainment. Elsie was very fond of ballads, and I could hardly please her better than by bringing a new one with me. But in default of that, an old one or a story would be welcomed. There were very few books to be had then in that part of the country, and therefore any mode of literature was precious. The schoolmaster was the chief source of such provisions, and this evening I recited a ballad of his.

"That's not a bad ballad," said James Duff, when I had finished. "Have you a tune it would go to, Elsie?"

But she and Turkey were looking at each other, and did not hear. James Duff began to talk to me, and Elsie began putting away the supper things. In a few minutes I missed her and Turkey, and they were absent for some time. Then, as the night was growing quite stormy, James Duff counselled our return, and we obeyed.

I saw Elsie at church most Sundays. Sometimes I had a word with her when we came out, but my father expected us to walk home with him, and generally Turkey walked away with her.

CHAPTER THIRTY-FOUR

More Schooling

I left home this summer for the first time, and followed my brother Tom to the grammar school in the county town, in order afterward to follow him to the University. There was so much novelty and expectation in the change, that I did not feel the separation from my father and the rest of my family much at first. That came afterward, but for the time, the pleasure of a long ride on the top of the mail-coach, with a bright sun and a pleasant breeze, the various incidents connected with changing horses and starting afresh, and then the outlook for the first peep of the sea, occupied my attention too thoroughly.

I worked fairly at the grammar school and got on well, but whether I should gain a scholarship remained doubtful. Before the time for the examination arrived, I went to spend a week at home. It was a great disappointment to me that I had to return again without seeing Elsie, but it could not be helped. The only Sunday I had there was a stormy day, late in October, and Turkey informed me that Elsie had a bad cold and could not be out. And with one thing and another, I was not able to go and see her.

Turkey was now doing a man's work on the farm, and stood high in everyone's estimation. He was a great favorite with Allister and Davie, and took very much the same place with the former as he had taken with me. I had lost nothing of my regard for him, and he urged me to diligence and thoroughness in my studies, pressing upon me that no one had ever done lasting work, "that is," Turkey would say, "work that goes to the making of the world," without being in earnest as to the *what* and conscientious as to the *how*.

"Don't try to be a great man," he said once. "You might succeed, and then find out you had failed altogether."

"How could that be, Turkey?" I objected. "A body can't succeed and fail both at once."

"A body might succeed," he replied, "in doing what he wanted to do, and then find out that it was not in the least what he had thought it."

"What rule are you to follow then, Turkey?"

"Just the rule of duty. What you ought to do, that you must do. Then when a choice comes—not involving duty—choose what you like best."

"Aren't you fit for something better than farm work yourself, Turkey?" I foolishly ventured to suggest.

"It's *my* work," said Turkey in a decisive tone, which left me no room for rejoinder.

This conversation took place in the barn, where Turkey happened to be thrashing alone that morning. In turning the sheaf, or in laying a fresh one, there was always a moment's pause in the din, and then only we talked, so that our conversation was a good deal broken. I had buried myself in the straw, as in days of old, to keep myself warm, and there I lay and looked at Turkey while he thrashed, and thought with myself that his face had grown much more solemn than it used to be. But when he did smile, all the old merry sweetness dawned again.

The next day I returned for the examination, was happy enough to gain a small scholarship, and entered on my first winter at college. My father wrote to me once a week or so, and occasionally I had a letter with more ink than matter in it from one of my younger brothers. Tom was now in Edinburgh in a lawyer's office. I had no correspondence with Turkey. Mr. Wilson wrote to me sometimes, and along with good advice would occasionally send me some verses, but he told me little or nothing of any news from home.

CHAPTER THIRTY-FIVE

The End of Boyhood

On a Saturday morning in the following April, I boarded the mail coach to return home for the summer. The sky was bright, with great fleecy clouds sailing over it, from which now and then fell a shower in large drops. The wind was keen, and I had to wrap myself well in my cloak. But my heart was light, and full of the pleasure of ended and successful labor, of home-going, and the signs of sun and sky that summer was at hand.

Five months had gone by since I last left home, and it had seemed such an age to Davie, that he burst out crying when he saw me. My father received me with a certain tenderness which seemed to grow upon him. Kirsty followed Davie's example, and Allister, without saying much, haunted me like my shadow. I saw nothing of Turkey that evening.

In the morning we went to church, where I sat beside the reclining stone warrior, from whose face age had nearly worn the features away. I gazed at him, and there grew upon me a strange solemnity, a sense of the passing away of earthly things, and a strong conviction of the need of something that could not pass. This feeling lasted all the time of the service, and increased while I lingered in the church until my father should come out of the vestry.

I stood in the passage, leaning against the tomb. A cloud came over the sun, and the whole church grew dark as a December day—gloomy and cheerless. I heard two old women talking together. The pulpit was between us, but I peeped around and saw them.

"And when did it happen, said you?" asked one of them,

whose head moved incessantly with palsy.

"About two o'clock this morning," answered the other, who leaned on a stick, almost bent double with rheumatism. "I saw their next-door neighbor this morning, and he had seen Jamie. But as William is a Seceder, nobody's been to tell the minister, and I'm just waiting to let him know, for she was a great favorite of his. Nobody thought it would come so sudden like. When I saw her mother last, there was no such notion in her head."

Just then my father came up the aisle from the vestry, and stopped to speak to the old women.

"Elsie Duff's gone, poor thing!" said the rheumatic one.

What followed I have forgotten. The sound was in my ears, and my body seemed to believe it, though my soul could not comprehend it. When I came to myself I was alone in the church, standing beside the monument, leaning on the carved Crusader. The sun was again shining, and the old church was full of light. But the sunshine had changed for me, and I felt very mournful. I should see the sweet face and hear the lovely voice no more in this world. I endeavored to realize the thought, but could not, and I left the church hardly conscious of anything but a dull sense of loss.

My father was very grave, and spoke tenderly of Elsie— but he did not know how much I had loved her, and I could not make much response. I think too that he said less than he otherwise would, from the fear of calling back to my mind too vivid a memory of how ill I had once behaved to her. It was, indeed, my first thought the moment he uttered her name, but it soon passed, for much had come between that time and this.

In the evening I went up to the farm to look for Turkey, who had not been at church either morning or afternoon. He was the only one I could talk to about Elsie. He was bedding the cows, with his back toward me when I entered.

"Turkey," I said.

He looked around with a slow mechanical motion, with a conscious effort of the will. His face was so white, and wore such a look of loss, that it terrified me like the presence of something awful. I stood speechless. He looked at me for a moment, and then came slowly up to me, and laid his hand on my shoulder.

"Ranald," he said, "we were to have been married next year."

Before the grief of the man, mighty in its silence, my whole being was humbled. I knew my love was not so great as his. It grew in my eyes a pale and feeble thing, and I felt worthless in the presence of the dead, whom alive I had loved with a peaceful gladness. Elsie belonged to Turkey, and he had lost her, and his heart was breaking. I threw my arms around him, and wept for him, not for myself.

It was thus I ceased to be a boy—and here, therefore, my boyhood story ends.

Before I returned to the university, Turkey had enlisted and left the place. My father's half-prophecy concerning him is now fulfilled: he is a general. I have never seen him or heard from him since he left my father's service, but I am confident that if ever we meet, it will be as old and true friends.

Bacon: Francis Bacon, 1561-1626. English writer, philosopher, and politician; author of *Essays*.

bilberries: The blue-black fruit of a small English and European shrub.

bunghole: The cork hole in the side of a wooden barrel.

Catechism: A formal series of questions and answers used for instruction in the basics of the Christian religion. There is both a Longer and a Shorter Catechism.

claymore: Gaelic for "great sword." A double-edged sword used in the Scottish Highlands.

deal: A plank or board sawn from a log.

dirk: A small dagger.

dormer window: An upright window projecting from the roof of a house.

Andrew Ferrara: Another name for the claymore.

form: A wooden bench.

furlong: One-eighth of a mile.

furze: An evergreen with spines and yellow flowers.

Gaelic: The language spoken by the Celtic people of the Scottish Highlands.

garrett: A room in the attic or top floor of a house.

gimlet: A tool used for boring holes.

Jew's harp: A simple musical instrument, played by holding its metal frame in one's mouth and twanging a metal "tongue" with one's finger.

list: Strip of cloth or fabric.

Milton: John Milton, 1608-1674. Author of *Paradise Lost,*

Paradise Regained, and other religious poems.

Moloch: Ammonite god of fire, to whom children were sacrificed. (Leviticus 20:1-5)

paraphrases: Church of Scotland hymns based on Scripture.

peat: A thick mossy layer of decayed plants which forms peat bogs. In Scotland, peat was often cut into small pieces, dried, and burned as fuel.

pennons: A narrow flag or banner, often flown from the head of a knight's lance.

plaid: A thick tartan blanket worn as a cloak in Scotland.

press: A recessed cupboard holding food and dishes.

ricks: Stacks of hay or corn.

runnel: The channel of a brook or stream.

skene dubh: Gaelic for "black knife." A Scottish Highlander's knife, often carried in the stocking.

tow: Rough, unspun wool or flax.

Virgil: Roman poet, 70 B.C.–19 B.C.; author of *The Aeneid.*

weir: A dam which traps water to drive a mill wheel.

Winner Books are produced by Victor Books and are designed to entertain and instruct young readers in Christian principles.

Other Winner Books you will enjoy:
The Mystery Man of Horseshoe Bend
    by Linda Boorman
The Drugstore Bandit of Horseshoe Bend
    by Linda Boorman
The Hairy Brown Angel and Other Animal Tails
    edited by Grace Fox Anderson
The Peanut Butter Hamster and Other Animal Tails
    edited by Grace Fox Anderson
Skunk for Rent and Other Animal Tails
    edited by Grace Fox Anderson
The Incompetent Cat and Other Animal Tails
    edited by Grace Fox Anderson
The Duck Who Had Goosebumps and Other Animal Tails
    edited by Grace Fox Anderson
The Mysterious Prowler by Frances Carfi Matranga
The Forgotten Treasure by Frances Carfi Matranga
The Mystery of the Missing Will by Frances Carfi Matranga
The Hair-Pulling Bear Dog by Lee Roddy
The City Bear's Adventures by Lee Roddy
Dooger, the Grasshopper Hound by Lee Roddy
The Ghost Dog of Stoney Ridge by Lee Roddy
Mad Dog of Lobo Mountain by Lee Roddy
The Legend of the White Raccoon by Lee Roddy
The Boyhood of Ranald Bannerman
    by George MacDonald
The Genius of Willie MacMichael by George MacDonald
The Wanderings of Clare Skymer by George MacDonald